RAPE ON CAMPUS

Other Books in the At Issue Series:

RAPE ON CAMPUS

David Bender, *Publisher*
Bruno Leone, *Executive Editor*

Katie de Koster, *Managing Editor*
Scott Barbour, *Series Editor*

Bruno Leone, *Book Editor*
Katie de Koster, *Assistant Editor*

An Opposing Viewpoints Series®

Greenhaven Press, Inc.
San Diego, California

Library of Congress Cataloging-in-Publication Data

At issue : rape on campus / Bruno Leone and Katie de Koster, book
    editors.
        p.   cm. — (At issue series)
    Includes bibliographical references (p.) and index.
    ISBN 1-56510-296-7 (lib. bdg.) — ISBN 1-56510-263-0 (pbk.).
    1. Rape—United States. 2. Acquaintance rape—United States.
3. Women college students—Crimes against—United States. I. Leone,
Bruno, 1939- . II. de Koster, Katie, 1948- . III. Title: Rape on campus.
IV. Series.
HV6561.A88   1995   94-42400
364.1′532′0973—dc20   CIP

© 1995 by Greenhaven Press, Inc., PO Box 289009,
San Diego, CA 92198-9009

Printed in the U.S.A.

Table of Contents

Introduction

In 1990, a feminist group from Antioch College demanded that the administration of the college institute a sexual consent policy binding upon all Antioch students. The group, Womyn of Antioch, sought the policy out of frustration after two rapes were reported that year on campus, neither of which was prosecuted. To demonstrate their resolve, they threatened the college with "radical, physical actions" if their demands were not met. The campus furor instigated by the Womyn of Antioch resulted in a formal "Sexual Consent Policy," issued in 1992.

Drawn up by a committee of students, faculty, and administrators, the policy was primarily designed to prevent and—when that failed—deal with sexual offenses on campus. The process by which the plan would realize its purpose was quite straightforward. One party involved in an intimate encounter would be required to obtain the consent of the other party before the encounter could advance further. Should consent be given and the encounter escalate in intimacy, consent would be required at every level of intimacy. The need for graduated consent is clearly and unequivocally mandated on page one of the policy:

> If the level of sexual intimacy increases during an interaction (i.e., if two people move from kissing while fully clothed—which is one level—to undressing for direct physical contact, which is another level), the people involved need to express their clear verbal consent before moving to that new level. If one person wants to *initiate* moving to a higher level of sexual intimacy in an interaction, *that person is responsible for getting the verbal consent of the other person(s) involved before moving to that level.*

The principle behind the Antioch policy is simple both in theory and practice. If someone consents to an intimate act at any and every level of intimacy, he or she cannot claim rape after the fact. However, if someone refuses to consent, then any intimate act following the refusal can be labeled as forcible sex and dealt with accordingly.

As word of the policy escaped the campus of the small (650 students) liberal arts college in Yellow Springs, Ohio, the unexpected occurred. Journalists of all political persuasions, both wags and the more serious minded, set upon the Antioch plan with a relish usually reserved for reports of wayward royalty. What ordinarily would have remained a local affair became, with almost comedic effect, a national media event. Ignoring the purpose of the plan, most commentators chose to focus instead upon the process, namely, the need for consent. Typical of the comments was an article by Jeffrey Hart that appeared in the conservative publication *Human Events*. Homing in on the specificity of the Antioch rules, Hart wrote that "if you undo a button without verbal permission, then the director of the Sexual Prevention and Survivor Advocacy Program has got you in his or her claws." Not to be outdone by written derision, the

7

New Yorker ridiculed the Antioch plan with a cartoon in which Dracula intones to his young victim: "And now may I bite your neck?"

However, not all reactions to the Antioch Sexual Consent Policy were negative. In a campus publication, Alan E. Guskin, the president of Antioch, while acknowledging that "there has been criticism and much fun poked at Antioch's policy," quoted a letter that appeared in the November 29, 1993, issue of the *New Yorker*. In it, the writer praises the policy as a "subtle and imaginative mandate" providing undergraduates with an opportunity "to discover that wordplay and foreplay can be happily entwined." Others agree with Eric Fassin, a professor at New York University, who argues that the Antioch rules "help dispel the illusion that sexuality is a state of nature individuals must experience outside the social contract, and that eroticism cannot exist within the conventions of language."

In reality, the Antioch Policy and the turbulence fomented in its wake are a reaction to and an indication of what is perceived by many as a growing blight on America's campuses: an unconscionable number of sexual assaults on female students. In 1982, *Ms.* magazine obtained a $267,000 grant from the National Institute of Mental Health to conduct a nationwide survey to determine the degree to which sexual assaults on college campuses do occur. *Ms.* commissioned Mary Koss, a psychiatry professor at the University of Arizona, to conduct the survey, named the Campus Project on Sexual Assault. After a comprehensive three-year study, which included a "Sexual Experiences Survey" administered to 8,159 college students throughout the United States, Koss announced that "25 percent of women in college have been the victims of rape or attempted rape." In their book *Sexual Assault on Campus*, Carol Bohmer and Andrea Parrot claim that the 25 percent figure declared in the Koss study still prevails. They argue that "data from recent studies done nationally reveal that between 20 and 25 percent of college women have experienced forced sex (including rape, oral sex, anal sex, and other forms of penetration) at some time during their college careers." Although it is a decade old, the Koss study is still widely heralded as illustrative of the extent of the campus rape problem.

The results of the Koss study have been challenged by many. It is widely argued that Mary Koss and her supporters redefined sexual deviancy to include categories of behavior that had not previously been characterized as forcible rape. As a result, the statistics revealing a high percentage of sexual assaults on campus may be, at best, unreliable and inaccurate. Charles Krauthammer, a contributing editor of the *New Republic*, argues this point in the March/April 1994 issue of *Current*. He writes:

> Rape has been expanded by Koss and other researchers to include behavior that you and I would not recognize as rape. And not just you and I—the supposed victims themselves do not recognize it as rape. In the Koss study, 73 percent of the women she labeled as rape victims did not consider themselves to have been raped. Fully 42 percent had further sexual relations with the so-called rapist.

Despite the polemics, there is one aspect of the campus rape issue upon which most would probably agree: Whatever the number of rapes, the majority of perpetrators go untried and unpunished. Although it is widely recognized that sexual assaults on college campuses do occur with some frequency, the numbers of reported cases of rape remain small; and of those brought to the attention of campus authorities, the number that eventuate in judicial proceedings is far smaller still. There are many reasons for this. Historically, campus authorities have been reticent to take action, convinced that it might give rise to bad publicity directed at the college and ultimately reflect poorly upon the authorities themselves. Moreover, large numbers of victims tend to remain silent, fearing that they themselves may be accused of provoking the rape. Additional victim fears include the possibility of reprisals by the accused and of being stigmatized by the entire college community. Finally, the majority of victims are not willing to undergo the trauma and publicity of a rape hearing on campus when experience whispers that assailants often get off without even a mild rebuke.

The extent of the problem of sexual assault, both on campus and in the nation at large, is evidenced by the growing media attention focusing upon sexual crimes, as well as the large number of colleges and universities that have begun instituting programs and policies to prevent and prosecute campus rape. *At Issue: Rape on Campus* offers the reader a spectrum of opinions drawn from within and without academia dealing with the issue of campus rape and the broader issue of rape in society.

1

Antioch College:
A Sexual Consent Policy

The Antioch College Community

The Antioch College Sexual Consent Policy was written by a committee of students, faculty, and administrators of Antioch College and approved by the college's Administrative Council. Antioch College is in Yellow Springs, Ohio.

In response to the increasing frequency of sexual violence on college campuses, the community (students, faculty, and administration) of Antioch College has developed a plan to both define and deal with sexual harassment and other sexual offenses on campus. The plan provides students with guidelines for determining what constitutes a sexual offense and what to do when one has occurred, and outlines possible punishments for the offender.

The statistics on the frequency of sexual violence on college campuses today are alarming. While we try to make Antioch a safe environment for everyone, we still have problems here. There is date and acquaintance rape, and stranger rape, and, while the majority of perpetrators are men and the majority of victims are women, there are also female perpetrators and male victims. There are also many students who have already experienced sexual violence before arriving at Antioch; healing from that experience may be an integral part of their personal, social and academic lives while they are here.

Antioch has a Sexual Offense Prevention and Survivor's Advocacy Program which consists of an Advocate and trained Peer Advocates and Educators. They can talk with you confidentially about any questions or concerns you have, provide or arrange for counseling, and help you access resources about healing from sexual violence. They also provide advocacy for rape victims dealing with a hospital, police, the courts, and/or campus administrative procedures.

Antioch has two policies, a sexual harassment policy and a sexual offense policy, which have been designed to help deal with these problems when they occur on campus and/or when they involve an Antioch community member. Read these policies; you are held responsible for knowing them. Under the sexual offense policy:

The Antioch College Sexual Offense Policy, Administrative Council of Antioch College, 1992. Reprinted with permission.

- All sexual contact and conduct between any two people must be consensual;
- Consent must be obtained verbally before there is any sexual contact or conduct;
- If the level of sexual intimacy increases during an interaction (i.e., if two people move from kissing while fully clothed—which is one level—to undressing for direct physical contact, which is another level), the people involved need to express their clear verbal consent before moving to that new level;
- If one person wants to *initiate* moving to a higher level of sexual intimacy in an interaction, *that person is responsible for getting the verbal consent of the other person(s) involved before moving to that level;*
- If you have had a particular level of sexual intimacy before with someone, you must still ask each and every time;
- If you have a sexually transmitted disease, you must disclose it to a potential sexual partner.

Don't ever make any assumptions about consent; they can hurt someone and get you in trouble. Also, do not take silence as consent; it isn't. Consent must be clear and verbal (i.e., saying: yes, I want to kiss you also).

Special precautions are necessary if you, or the person with whom you would like to be sexual, are under the influence of alcohol, drugs, or prescribed medication. Extreme caution should always be used. Consent, even verbal consent, may not be meaningful. Taking advantage of someone who is "under the influence" is never acceptable behavior. If, for instance, you supply someone with alcohol and get her/him drunk so that person will consent to have sex with you (figuring you wouldn't get "as far" if that person were sober), then their consent may be meaningless and you may be charged under the sexual offense policy. If you are so drunk that you act with someone totally inappropriately (in a way maybe you wouldn't if you were sober), of if you are so drunk you don't hear "no," you may still be charged under the sexual offense policy.

If sexual contact and/or conduct is not mutually and simultaneously initiated, then the person who initiates sexual contact/conduct is responsible for getting the verbal consent of the other individual(s) involved.

If you have a hard time knowing or setting your own personal boundaries, or respecting other people's boundaries, you may have a harder time if alcohol or drugs are involved. For truly consensual sex, you and your partner(s) should be sober to be sexual.

Sexual harassment should be reported to the Advocate; depending on the wishes of the complainant, mediation may be attempted or the charge may be referred to the Hearing Board. Other forms of sexual offenses are also reported to the Advocate, and depending on the wishes of the victim/survivor may be referred for mediation or to the Hearing Board which hears cases of sexual offenses where the alleged offender is a student. If the accused violator is not a student, the case may be referred for follow-up to the appropriate person. In cases of rape and sexual assault, reporting to law enforcement authorities is also encouraged. Anonymous reports may also be made. Complaint forms are in a box outside the program offices in Long Hall, or you can make a report directly to the Advocate. All reports are treated confidentially; every attempt is made to treat everyone involved fairly, and to honor the wishes of the victim regarding what is done (or not done).

If you are raped or sexually assaulted:

- Get somewhere safe.
- Contact a friend you trust, a hall advisor, or HAC and/or
- Contact a peer advocate or the Advocate directly, or through the Rape Crisis Line.
- You may also wish to notify the police.
- Do not bathe, change clothes, or otherwise clean-up yet.

The peer advocate or Advocate will provide emotional support, help you to understand your thoughts and feelings at the time, explain your options to you, and support you in whatever decisions you choose to make.

If you have been sexually harassed at a co-op site, tell your co-op advisor and the Advocate.

If you have been victimized sexually in the past and you would like some assistance in working on these issues, there is help available. See a counselor at the Counseling Center or contact the Advocate or a peer advocate. If it's appropriate for you to see a therapist off-campus, we will try to help you find someone suitable. There are also support groups available each term for men and women who are survivors of sexual abuse.

There are ways to help prevent sexual violence on campus. A few tips:

- *Always* lock your room door when you're going to undress, sleep, or if you're under the influence of a substance which might impair your ability to react quickly. It's a good idea to get in the habit of locking your door whenever you're inside.
- *Never* prop outside doors open—strangers can enter buildings, as well as friends.
- If you're walking or running on the bike path at times when you might be the only one around, take a friend.
- Learn self-defense.
- Know your sexual desires and boundaries and communicate them clearly to any (potential) sexual partner; "listen" to your boundaries and honor them. If you're not sure, say "no" rather than "yes" or "maybe."
- Ask what a (potential) sexual partner's desires and boundaries are; listen to and respect them.
- If someone violates a sexual boundary, confront him/her on it. That may mean telling them directly, or, as a first step, talking with your hall advisor or HAC, the Advocate or a peer advocate, a counselor, or the Dean of Students.

The Antioch College Sexual Offense Policy

All sexual contact and conduct on the Antioch College campus and/or occurring with an Antioch community member must be consensual.

When a sexual offense, as defined herein, is committed by a community member, such action will not be tolerated.

Antioch College provides and maintains educational programs for all community members, some aspects of which are required. The educational aspects of this policy are intended to prevent sexual offenses and ultimately to heighten community awareness.

In support of this policy and community safety, a support network exists that consists of the Sexual Offense Prevention and Survivors' Advocacy Program, an Advocate, Peer Advocates, and victim/survivor support groups through the Sexual Offense Prevention and Survivors' Advocacy Program and Counseling Services.

The Advocate (or other designated administrator) shall be responsible for initiation and coordination of measures required by this policy.

The implementation of this policy also utilizes established Antioch governance structures and adheres to contractual obligations.

Consent

1. For the purpose of this policy, "consent" shall be defined as follows: the act of willingly and verbally agreeing to engage in specific sexual contact or conduct.

2. If sexual contact and/or conduct is not mutually and simultaneously initiated, then the person who initiates sexual contact/conduct is responsible for getting the verbal consent of the other individual(s) involved.

3. Obtaining consent is an on-going process in any sexual interaction. Verbal consent should be obtained with each new level of physical and/or sexual contact/conduct in any given interaction, regardless of who initiates it. Asking "Do you want to have sex with me?" is not enough. The request for consent must be specific to each act.

4. The person with whom sexual contact/conduct is initiated is responsible to express verbally and/or physically her/his willingness or lack of willingness when reasonably possible.

5. If someone has initially consented but then stops consenting during a sexual interaction, she/he should communicate withdrawal verbally and/or through physical resistance. The other individual(s) must stop immediately.

6. To knowingly take advantage of someone who is under the influence of alcohol, drugs and/or prescribed medication is not acceptable behavior in the Antioch community.

7. If someone verbally agrees to engage in specific contact or conduct, but it is not of her/his own free will due to any of the circumstances stated in (a) through (d) below, then the person initiating shall be considered in violation of this policy if:

   a. the person submitting is under the influence of alcohol or other substances supplied to her/him by the person initiating;
   b. the person submitting is incapacitated by alcohol, drugs, and/or prescribed medication;
   c. the person submitting is asleep or unconscious;
   d. the person initiating has forced, threatened, coerced, or intimidated the other individual(s) into engaging in sexual contact and/or sexual conduct.

Offenses defined

The following sexual contact/conduct are prohibited under Antioch College's Sexual Offense Policy and, in addition to possible criminal prosecution, may result in sanctions up to and including expulsion or termination of employment.

Rape: Non-consensual penetration, however slight, of the vagina or anus; non-consensual fellatio or cunnilingus.

Sexual Assault: Non-consensual sexual conduct exclusive of vaginal and anal penetration, fellatio and cunnilingus. This includes, but is not limited to, attempted non-consensual penetration, fellatio, or cunnilingus; the respondent coercing or forcing the primary witness to engage in non-consensual sexual contact with the respondent or another.

Sexual Imposition: Non-consensual sexual contact. "Sexual contact" includes the touching of thighs, genitals, buttocks, the pubic region, or the breast/chest area.

Insistent and/or Persistent Sexual Harassment: Any insistent and/or persistent emotional, verbal or mental intimidation or abuse found to be sexually threatening or offensive. This includes, but is not limited to, unwelcome and irrelevant comments, references, gestures or other forms of personal attention which are inappropriate and which may be perceived as persistent sexual overtones or denigration.

Non-Disclosure of a Known Positive HIV Status: Failure to inform one's sexual partner of one's known positive HIV status prior to engaging in high risk sexual conduct.

Non-Disclosure of a Known Sexually Transmitted Disease: Failure to inform one's sexual partner of one's known infection with a sexually transmitted disease (other than HIV) prior to engaging in high risk sexual conduct.

Procedures

1. To maintain the safety of all community members, community members who are suspected of violating this policy should be made aware of the concern about their behavior. Sometimes people are not aware that their behavior is sexually offensive, threatening, or hurtful. Educating them about the effects of their behavior may cause them to change their behavior.

If someone suspects that a violation of this Sexual Offense Policy may have occurred, she/he should contact a member of the Sexual Offense Prevention and Survivors' Advocacy Program or the Dean of Students.

It is strongly encouraged that suspected violations be reported, and that they be reported as soon as is reasonable after a suspected violation has occurred. Where criminal misconduct is involved, reporting the misconduct to the local law enforcement agency is also strongly encouraged.

Any discussion of a suspected violation with a member of the Sexual Offense Prevention and Survivors' Advocacy Program or the Dean of Students will be treated as confidential.

2. When a suspected violation of this policy is reported, the person who receives the report with the Sexual Offense Prevention and Survivors' Advocacy Program or the Dean of Students office will explain to the person reporting all of her/his options (such as mediation, the Hearing Board, and criminal prosecution) which are appropriate to the suspected offense.

3. If the person reporting a suspected policy violation wishes to

arrange for mediation, then the Advocate, the Dean of Students, or a staff member of the Sexual Offense Prevention and Survivors' Advocacy program shall arrange for mediation consistent with the mediation guidelines used by the Sexual Offense Prevention and Survivors' Advocacy Program.

    a. If the Dean of Students arranges mediation, the Dean shall notify the Advocate of the mediation session.

    b. A written agreement with educational and/or behavioral requirements may be part of the outcome of a mediation session. Copies of this agreement shall be given to the parties involved, the Advocate and the Dean of Students.

    c. Should a student persist in sexually threatening or offensive behavior after mediation has been attempted, the Sexual Harassment Committee or the Advocate should refer the case to the Hearing Board.

    d. If a satisfactory conclusion is not reached through mediation, or if the mediation agreement is not adhered to by any of its participants, then the case may be referred to the Hearing Board.

4. In the event that an action taken by the Dean of Students regarding a sexual offense is appealed, the appeal shall be made to the Hearing Board.

5. If the primary witness wishes the Hearing Board to make a finding regarding an alleged policy violation, the primary witness must file a written complaint with the Advocate. The Advocate shall inform the primary witness of her/his rights regarding procedure and appeal under this policy.

There will be no reference to the past consensual, non-violent sexual contact and/or conduct of either the primary witness or the respondent.

---

6. When a written complaint is filed, if the respondent is an employee, the Advocate shall inform the President or the President's designee of the reported violation of the Sexual Offense Policy. The matter will be promptly investigated by the appropriate administrator or other supervisor with the assistance of the Advocate. If whatever review process appropriate to the employee results in a determination that the policy has been violated, then the remedy should be commensurate with the seriousness of the violation, and procedures specified in College and University policies should be followed.

7. When an official report is filed, if the respondent is a student, then the following procedures shall be followed:

    A. The Advocate shall notify the Dean of Students, or another senior College official, who shall have the respondent report to the Dean of Students' office within a reasonable period of time, not to exceed the next business day the College is open that the respondent is on campus. When the respondent reports, the respondent will then be informed by the Advocate and/or the Dean of Students of the report of the sexual offense, the policy violation which is being alleged, and her/his rights regarding procedure and appeal. The respondent will be given an opportunity to present her/his side of the story at that time. If the respondent does not report as directed, then implementation of this policy shall proceed.

B. Based on the information available, the Advocate, or the Dean of Students in the Advocate's absence, will determine whether there is reasonable cause to believe that a policy violation may have occurred.

C. In the event that the respondent is situated on campus, if (1) there is reasonable cause to believe that a policy violation may have occurred, and (2) there is reasonable cause to believe that the respondent may pose a threat or danger to the safety of the community, the Hearing Board will be convened as soon as possible, preferably within 24 hours from the time of the report to the Advocate, to determine whether the respondent shall be removed from campus until the conclusion of the Hearing process. If the Hearing Board cannot be convened within 24 hours but there is reasonable cause as stated in (1) and (2) above, the Dean of Students, or the Advocate in the Dean of Students' absence, can act to remove the respondent from campus.

If the respondent is living on-campus and is temporarily banned from campus, the College will help arrange housing if the respondent is unable to locate any on her/his own.

If the respondent is taking classes on-campus and is temporarily banned from attending classes, the College will help provide alternative instruction.

The emergency removal of the respondent from campus shall not constitute a determination that the respondent has violated this policy.

D. The Hearing Board will then convene for a Hearing, to hear the case. Consistent with this policy, the Hearing Board will take into account the primary witness's story, the respondent's story, witnesses, the past history of the respondent, and other relevant evidence, and will determine whether or not a policy violation has occurred and which aspect of the policy has been violated.

E. The Hearing shall take place as soon thereafter as is reasonable, no longer than seven days from the date of filing or the notification of the respondent, whichever is later, unless the Advocate determines that reasonable cause exists for convening the meeting at a later, still reasonable time, in which event the Advocate shall so notify the Chair of the Hearing Board.

F. If the primary witness chooses, she/he may have a representative at all hearings of the Hearing Board and/or through any appeals process. The primary witness's advocate is to provide advocacy and emotional support for the primary witness. When appropriate, if the primary witness chooses, the Advocate or a Peer Advocate may act as the primary witness's representative at all hearings of the Hearing Board and/or through any appeals process. The primary witness may also choose to have someone outside the Sexual Offense Prevention and Survivors' Advocacy Program serve as her/his representative. Choosing a representative from within the Antioch community is encouraged.

G. If the respondent chooses, she/he may have a representative at all hearings of the Hearing Board and/or through any appeals process. The respondent's advocate is to provide advocacy and emotional support for the respondent. When appropriate, if the respondent chooses, the respondent may select an advocate from the list maintained by the Dean of Students' office of administrators and tenured faculty who have agreed to serve in this role. This advocate may act as the respondent's representative at all hearings of the Hearing Board and/or through any appeals process.

The respondent may also choose to have someone outside this list serve as her/his representative. Choosing a representative from within the Antioch community is encouraged.

8. The Hearing Board and any appellate body which hears a case under this policy shall administer its proceedings according to these fundamental assumptions:

A. There will be no reference to the past consensual, non-violent sexual contact and/or conduct of either the primary witness or the respondent.
B. No physical evidence of a sexual offense is necessary to determine that one has occurred, nor is a visit to the hospital or the administration of a rape kit required. The primary witness shall be supported by the Advocate in whatever decisions she/he makes, and be informed of legal procedures regarding physical evidence.
C. The fact that a respondent was under the influence of drugs or alcohol or mental dysfunction at the time of the sexual offense will not excuse or justify the commission of any sexual offense as defined herein, and shall not be used as a defense.

9. This policy is intended to deal with sexual offenses which occurred in the Antioch community, and/or with an Antioch community member, on or after February 7, 1991. Sexual offenses which occurred prior to that date were still a violation of community standards, and should be addressed through the policies and governance structures which were in effect at the time of the offense.

The Hearing Board

1. The Hearing Board's duties are:
   a. to hear all sides of the story;
   b. to investigate as appropriate;
   c. to determine if a violation of this policy has occurred;
   d. to develop, in consultation with the Dean of Students and the Advocate, an appropriate remedy in cases where mandatory remedies are not prescribed in this policy;
   e. to prepare a written report setting forth its findings which it distributes to the parties involved and the Dean of Students.

2. The Hearing Board will consist of three community representatives as voting members and the Dean of Students as an ex-officio member.

3. By the end of each Spring quarter, nine representatives will be chosen to form a Hearing Board pool to begin serving at the beginning of the next academic year (fall quarter) for the duration of that academic year: three each from the categories of students, faculty, and administrators/staff members.

A. The nine members of the Hearing Board pool shall be appointed by ADCIL from the following recommended candidates:

1. Six students recommended by COMCIL;
2. Six faculty members recommended by the Dean of Faculty and FEC;
3. Six administrators/staff members who shall be recommended by the President of the College.

B. At least five members of the Hearing Board pool shall be women.

C. Three of the representatives shall be appointed by ADCIL to serve each quarter as a Hearing Board. One Hearing Board member must be from each of the three categories listed above, and at least one member must be a person of color.

For every case which is heard, at least one Hearing Board member must be the same sex as the primary witness, and at least one Hearing Board member must be the same sex as the respondent.

D. One member of the Hearing Board shall be designated by ADCIL to serve as Chair. The Chair shall preside for all Hearing Board meetings that quarter, and shall make the necessary physical arrangements to convene the Hearing Board (i.e., contact Hearing Board members, notify all parties involved of date, time, place, etc.,)

E. The six representatives who are not serving in a particular quarter shall be alternates in case an active member is not available or has a conflict of interest.

F. If an active member of the Hearing Board has a conflict of interest in the case, that member is responsible to report the conflict as soon as possible. ADCIL shall be responsible to determine if the conflict requires replacing the member, with an alternate chosen by ADCIL to immediately take her/his place. If convening ADCIL for this purpose would serve to delay the Hearing Board process, then the President shall make a determination regarding conflict and, if necessary, appoint an alternate.

4. All members of the Hearing Board pool shall receive training by the Advocate and the College attorney regarding this policy and pertinent legal issues.

5. The Hearing Board is expected to follow the procedures outlined in Appendix D. Any procedures not covered in this policy, including Appendix D, shall be determined according to the discretion of the Hearing Board.

Remedies

1. When a policy violation by a student is found by the Hearing Board, the Hearing Board shall also determine a remedy which is commensurate with the offense, except in those cases where mandatory remedies are prescribed in this policy.

When a remedy is not prescribed, the Hearing Board shall determine the remedy in consultation with the Dean of Students and the Advocate, and shall include an educational and/or rehabilitation component as part of the remedy.

2. *For Rape:* In the event that the Hearing Board determines that the violation of rape has occurred, as defined under this policy, then the re-

spondent must be expelled immediately.

3. *For Sexual Assault:* In the event that the Hearing Board determines that the violation of sexual assault has occurred, as defined under this policy, then the respondent must: (a) be suspended immediately for a period of no less than six months; (b) successfully complete a treatment program for sexual offenders approved by the Director of Counseling Services before returning to campus; and (c) upon return to campus, be subject to mandatory class and co-op scheduling so that the respondent and primary witness avoid, to the greatest extent possible, all contact, unless the primary witness agrees otherwise.

In the event that the Hearing Board determines that a second violation of sexual assault has occurred, with the same respondent, then the respondent must be expelled immediately.

When a policy violation by a student is found by the Hearing Board, the Hearing Board shall also determine a remedy which is commensurate with the offense.

---

4. *For Sexual Imposition:* In the event that the Hearing Board determines that the violation of sexual imposition has occurred, as defined under this policy, then the recommended remedy is that the respondent: (a) be suspended immediately for a period of no less than three months; (b) successfully complete a treatment program for sexual offenders approved by the Director of Counseling Services before returning to campus; and (c) upon return to campus, be subject to mandatory class and co-op scheduling so that the respondent and primary witness avoid, to the greatest extent possible, all contact, unless the primary witness agrees otherwise.

In the event that the Hearing Board determines that a second violation of sexual imposition has occurred, with the same respondent, then the recommended remedy is that the respondent: (a) be suspended immediately for a period of no less than six months; (b) successfully complete a treatment program for sexual offenders approved by the Director of Counseling Services before returning to campus; and (c) upon return to campus, be subject to mandatory class and co-op scheduling so that the respondent and primary witness avoid, to the greatest extent possible, all contact, unless the primary witness agrees otherwise.

In the event that the Hearing Board determines that a third violation of sexual imposition has occurred, with the same respondent, then the respondent must be expelled immediately.

5. *For Insistent and/or Persistent Sexual Harassment:* In the event that the Hearing Board determines that the violation of insistent and/or persistent sexual harassment has occurred, as defined under this policy, then the recommended remedy is that the respondent: (a) be suspended immediately for a period of no less than six months; (b) successfully complete a treatment program for sexual offenders approved by the Director of Counseling Services before returning to campus; and (c) upon return to campus, be subject to mandatory class and co-op scheduling so that the respondent and primary witness avoid, to the greatest extent possible, all contact, unless the primary witness agrees otherwise.

In the event that the Hearing Board determines that a second violation of insistent and/or persistent sexual harassment has occurred, with the same respondent, then the respondent must be expelled immediately.

6. *For Non-Disclosure of a Known Positive HIV Status:* In the event that the Hearing Board determines that there has been non-disclosure of a known positive HIV status, as defined under this policy, then the recommended remedy is that the respondent be expelled immediately.

7. *For Non-Disclosure of a Known Sexually Transmitted Disease:* In the event that the Hearing Board determines that there has been non-disclosure of a known sexually transmitted disease, as defined under this policy, then the recommended remedy is that the respondent be suspended immediately for a period of no less than three months.

In the event that the Hearing Board determines that there has been a second failure to disclose one's known sexually transmitted disease, as defined under this policy, then the recommended remedy is that the respondent be suspended immediately for a period of no less than six months.

In the event that the Hearing Board determines that there has been a third failure to disclose one's known sexually transmitted disease, as defined under this policy, then the recommended remedy is that the respondent be expelled immediately.

8. In all cases, *a second offense* under this policy, regardless of category, must receive a more severe consequence than did the first offense if the second offense occurred after the Hearing Board's first finding of a respondent's violation of this policy.

9. The remedy for *a third offense* of this policy, regardless of category, must be expulsion, if the third offense occurred after the Hearing Board's first or second finding of a respondent's violation of this policy.

10. It is the responsibility of the Dean of Students to ensure that the Hearing Board's remedies are carried out.

The appeals process

1. In the event that the respondent or primary witness is not satisfied with the decision of the Hearing Board, then she/he shall have the right to appeal the Hearing Board's decision within seventy-two hours of receiving that decision.

2. In the event of an appeal, the College shall secure the services of a hearing review officer with experience in conducting arbitrations or administrative agency or other informal hearings. A hearing review officer, who is not a current member of the Antioch College community, shall be selected by ADCIL in consultation with the Advocate for the purpose of handling such appeals.

3. The hearing review officer shall review the record(s) and/or written report(s) of the Hearing, any briefs or other written materials supplied to her/him by any of the involved parties, and meet with any of the involved parties which she/he determines appropriate, to determine if there was fundamental fairness in the Hearing process.

The hearing review officer's analysis shall include a determination of whether the respondent was fully apprised of the charges against her/him; that the appealing party had a full and fair opportunity to tell her/his side of the story; and whether there was any malfeasance by the Hearing Board. The hearing review officer will present her/his finding and recommendation for action, if any, to the President of the College.

Confidentiality

1. All of the proceedings of the Hearing Board, and all testimony given, shall be kept confidential.

2. For the duration of the Hearing process and any appeals process, the primary witness, the respondent, and any witnesses coming forward shall have the right to determine when and if their names are publicly released. No one shall make a public release of a name not their own while the process is underway. Any public breach of confidentiality may constitute a violation of community standards and be presented to the Community Standards Board for debate.

    A. The name of the primary witness shall not be considered public knowledge until such time that the primary witness releases her/his name publicly.

    B. The name of the respondent shall not be considered public knowledge until such time that the respondent releases her/his name publicly, unless the respondent is found in violation of the policy, at which time the release of the respondent's name may be included with the release of the Hearing Board's findings. The name of the respondent will be released with the Hearing Board's findings if a violation is found and the remedy includes the suspension or expulsion of the respondent.

    C. The names of any witnesses who testify to the Hearing Board shall not be released publicly until such time that each witness chooses to release her/his own name publicly.

3. In the event of an appeal, the appealing party (or the party considering the appeal) shall have the right to review any written and/or audio records of the hearing. Such review shall take place on the Antioch campus with a member of the Hearing Board present. No materials are to be duplicated by any party; no materials are to be removed from the Antioch campus except to be given to the hearing review officer or to the College attorneys.

4. All members of the Hearing Board, including any note-takers, are bound to keep the contents of the proceedings confidential.

5. All written and/or audio records of the process which are kept by the Hearing Board are to be turned over to the College Attorneys at the conclusion of the appeals process, and shall be stored in their offices, to be disposed of when and as they see fit.

Educational and support implementation procedures

1. A minimum of one educational workshop about sexual offenses, consent, and the nature of sexual offenses as they pertain to this policy will be incorporated into each quarterly orientation program for new students. This workshop shall be conducted by the Advocate or by a person designated by the Advocate. Attendance shall be required of all students new to the Antioch community.

2. Workshops on sexual offense issues will also be offered during all study quarters. The content of these workshops shall be determined by the Advocate. Each student shall be required to attend at least one workshop each academic year for which she/he is on campus for one or more study quarters, effective Fall 1992. Attendance records shall be maintained, and given to the Registrar's office. This requirement must be com-

pleted for graduation [pending approval by the faculty].

    a. It is recommended to the faculty that it develop a policy encouraging all faculty members to attend workshops on sexual offenses.

    b. Further, it is recommended to the College and University administration that all employees working on the Antioch College campus be encouraged to attend workshops on sexual offenses.

3. A one-credit P.E. self-defense course with an emphasis on women's self-defense will be offered each quarter. This course should be open to all Antioch community members free of charge.

4. Permanent support groups for female and male survivors of sexual offenses will be established and maintained through Counseling Services and/or the Sexual Offense Prevention and Survivors' Advocacy Program.

5. A Peer Advocacy Program will be maintained that shall consist of both female and male community members, recruited and trained by the Advocate. The Peer Advocate shall provide information and emotional support for sexual offense victims/survivors and primary witnesses. The peer advocates shall work with the Advocate in educating the community about sexual offenses and sexual wellness.

6. A support network for students who are on Co-op will be maintained by the Advocate and the Sexual Offense Prevention and Survivors' Advocacy Program, with trained crisis contact people available.

2

A Response to Critics of Antioch's Sexual Consent Policy

Alan E. Guskin

Alan E. Guskin was president of Antioch College in Yellow Springs, Ohio, when this article was written. He is currently chancellor of Antioch University.

There has been wide criticism leveled by the national press at Antioch College's Sexual Consent Policy. Because the Antioch Policy requires verbal consent prior to a sexual episode, it should not be considered repressive. Rather, it creates a situation where both parties involved in a sexual encounter are fully aware of the limits to which that encounter should be carried. In this way, it fosters a healthy social environment where consent eliminates the possibility of alleged coercion.

"Playing By The Antioch's Rules" (*New York Times* Op-Ed, December 26, 1993); "No Huggy, No Kissy at this School" (Associated Press, September 9, 1993); "The Eyes May Say Yes, But the Lips Have to Give Ok" (*USA Today*, September 10-12, 1993); "Antioch Sets New Standard of Sexual Equality" (*Boston Globe*, Ellen Goodman, September 23, 1993); all newspaper headlines challenging the reader about a two-year-old sexual consent policy at a small liberal arts college in Ohio. National attention for a college policy, even one about sex, is hard to believe. None of the stories were reporting on rape, sexual deviance, violence or any sordid behavior; they were reporting on an educational policy dealing with sexual interaction between students which states that students must seek verbal consent from a sexual partner at each level of sexual interaction.

National columnists wrote lengthy pieces, most making fun of the policy but a good number taking the sexual consent policy very seriously—Ellen Goodman devoted two thoughtful and positive columns exploring the new standard of sexual equality. The *New York Times*, the first major newspaper to visit the campus, devoted a thoughtful and well-written front-page article (September 25, 1993) to the policy after three full days of campus interviews with students and administrators, an edi-

Alan E. Guskin, *The Antioch Response: Sex, You Just Don't Talk About It*, published March 21, 1994. Reprinted with permission.

23

torial (October 11, 1993), a full column in the Sunday magazine, an op-ed piece (Sunday, December 26, 1993), and two positive letters from read-ers. *Saturday Night Live* satirizes the policy. *Time* magazine quoted verba-tim from the policy, more to make fun of it but with some element of seriousness; the *Washington Post*, after printing an opinion piece by me, sends an inept reporter who sensationalizes the issue beyond recognition.

Newsweek twice dealt with Antioch's policy; once as part of a piece challenging "sexual correctness," and in a separate piece on the College which portrays the students as sexually active but very much committed to the mutual sexual consent policy. In the style of *Newsweek*, and most of the media, there is an emphasis on sensationalizing the sexual behav-ior of some students as if it were representative of all students.

> *Today, the sexual freedom concerns of college stu-dents are not about having sex, but who controls sexual relationships.*

Front-page stories appeared in the *London Times* and *Bangkok Post*, as well as other newspapers in a number of countries and crews arrived from Swiss Television, Australian *60 Minutes* and the British Broadcasting Cor-poration. Stories appeared in almost every major newspaper in the United States and numerous local papers. There were scores of live interviews and discussions on radio and TV talk shows. TV reports appeared on every ma-jor network including a segment on *Eye to Eye with Connie Chung*, and a CNN report that ran continuously one weekend.

Daily, for over three months, television news cameras, reporters, pro-ducers, and photographers roamed the small campus searching for yet a new "angle" on this story. One national reporter, even more cynical than the rest, couldn't quite believe the two days of interviews with students and their near uniform acceptance of "their" policy.

I received irate letters—some unsigned, some from alumni, mostly from men—absurd, silly, outrageous: "I'm not going to give any more money." About one in five alums called as part of our fund-raising efforts reacted negatively—sometimes emotionally—to the policy. How can An-tioch, the bastion of freedom, do such a thing? I also received many pos-itive letters.

Wow! All this about a policy developed by students at a small college to deal with problems students are facing.

The public reaction is so out of keeping with the intentions of the stu-dents and others of us involved in the development of the policy that it cries out for discussion; why are people so upset by sexual consent? Why are so many so ready to reject the Antioch policy without any discussion with the people at Antioch? Why the nasty letters about a policy that only deals with campus life and developing standards for brief and tran-sitory sexual encounters of 18-to-25-year-olds in a college residential set-ting? Why the almost juvenile search for student modeling of the policy by so many TV reporters? Why the search for bizarre student behavior by many reporters only to sensationalize the behavior of a few students rather than accept the seriousness of the majority of Antioch students? And, more positive and interesting, why are the usually hardened na-tional reporters willing to spend time off the record sharing their views with me about sexual issues?

How can it be that this simple, explicit policy, developed by students for student sexual interaction, has become the most widely reported university news story on higher education in memory? How can the story continue in the national media for over four months? What deep seated feelings are touched, what issues joined?

Obviously, the reaction to the Antioch policy is all about sex! Surely, sex sells but these are only words, no pictures, no steamy narrative, only cold policy-type words. I believe it's not just sex that has created the reaction, but the Antioch requirement that students talk about sex! Talking about it with someone whom you desire; getting consent before having sex; having to think about sexual acts that you are about to do; communicating with a partner about your interests—outrageous, silly, anti-romantic, puritanical, unworkable, it will reduce men's desire.

While there has been criticism and much fun poked at Antioch's policy, there have also been many who support the notion of sexual consent, at colleges and universities throughout the country and in the media. A letter to the editor in *The New Yorker:*

> The November 29th Comment discusses Antioch College's rules requiring explicit verbal consent for each level of sexual intimacy. It is no punishment to put desire into words. Antioch's subtle and imaginative mandate is an erotic windfall: an opportunity for undergraduates to discover that wordplay and foreplay can be happily entwined; the chance to reinvent privately the joyless, overexposed arena called "sexual intimacy." What man or woman on Antioch's campus, or elsewhere, wouldn't welcome the direct question "May I kiss the hollow of your neck?" The possibilities are wonderful—pedagogic, even—as is the idea that language is choice.
>
> —*Julia A. Reidhead, New York City*

Antioch is a very special small college known for its innovative programs, its progressive values, its free-spirited students and its willingness to take risks. But this story is only partly about the open-mindedness of Antioch and its students. The reaction to this policy on sexual consent is more about the difficulty people—including reporters and editors—have understanding what is really happening to young people on our college and university campuses, even those who have children in college and who were sexually active themselves when they were students in the 1960s.

The 1990s and the 1960s/1970s

While critics and satirists may make points and cute statements, the pain of date rape and unhappy sexual encounters continue to tear campuses apart. Date rape is not a simple matter easily discounted by women's refusal to take responsibility for their own behavior or to accept the reality of a bad night. Whether one assumes that 10 or 25 percent of college women have experienced date rape, the reality is that many college women are experiencing serious abuse, that many college men are being abusive and sometimes accused and humiliated, and that the friends of each are suffering as well. Any campus policy that begins to deal with these difficulties and does it in a healthy, helpful manner is worthy of consideration.

National columnist Ellen Goodman reminds her readers in one of her two columns on the Antioch policy:

The point of the talk of sexual consent is, first of all, to protect women from violence. But the freedom from violence, from the fear of forced sex, is itself a first step towards sexual pleasure. Mutual sexual pleasure.

Freedom? Yes, the Antioch sexual consent policy is about individual freedom, just as the Antioch policies and perspectives in the 1950s, 1960s and 1970s were about individual freedom. Thirty to forty years ago the issue was student freedom from parental rules, where colleges and universities were setting themselves up as a controlling parent, establishing rules regarding sexual relationships. This led to the sexual experimentation of the 1960s. Sex on campus in the 1990s as compared to the 1960s is less mysterious to the sexually experienced high school graduates; after all, over two-thirds of all entering first-year students on campuses throughout the country have had sex prior to their arrival at college. Casual sexual interaction on campuses throughout the country is commonplace. Sex today is also more deadly due to AIDS.

Today, the sexual freedom concerns of college students are not about having sex, but who controls sexual relationships. The students of the 1990s were born in the 1970s amid the revolution for women's rights and freedoms. Most girls who grew into college-age women in the 1990s, have a very different conception of sexual encounters than their counterparts in the 1960s and 1970s and most of the men of the 1990s. Freedom for the 1990s woman is the freedom to determine how she uses her body. Women feel free to initiate sex and expect their partner to respect their desire to stop action whenever they choose. While the socialization of males has not kept pace with that of females, both genders are grappling with new roles in sexual behavior.

Sexuality as a defining issue

Sexual freedom of the 1990s is all about being able to have sexual relationships in the way that both people involved would like it to be. There is a great sense of security for each partner to know that their wishes will be honored and that they will not be accused of misinterpreting the other's sexual boundaries.

We must face directly what today's college students are telling us: that dealing with sexual matters in an open and direct manner is a defining issue for students of the 1990s. If there are doubts, a recent *USA Today* and MTV survey found that over 78 percent of the respondents who were between the ages of 16 and 29 thought that verbal consent regarding sexual behavior was desirable; the reason they gave was that such consent would help clear up miscommunication between partners. This finding held up for men (70 percent) and women (78 percent), African Americans (72 percent), Hispanics (82 percent) and whites (73 percent).

It is in this setting that sexual freedom and sexual consent are directly related to each other. To the man who thinks "why not?" in regards to sexual intercourse and the woman who thinks "why?", sexual consent means communication that leads each down the same path. That path, I believe, is more romantic and more passionate for both partners.

To the people who desire to satisfy themselves whether or not they are sure their partner feels the same way, sexual consent is not a freedom but a restraint. As one man at Antioch said when he first heard about the sexual consent policy, "This policy means I can't get what I want when I want it." He is right! But, is this freedom or license?

And then there is safe sex and AIDS. The freedom to be safe requires talking about past sexual behavior and about whether or not one's partner has AIDS or a sexually transmitted disease. It is also about being able to protect oneself with condoms even if it isn't the most romantic, passionate or comfortable thing. Talking about sex and sexual consent requires having to ask uncomfortable questions, but in the 1990s this is a life-saving skill.

The generation of the 1990s is confronting us with their sexuality. What would have been promiscuous behavior even in the 1960s is pretty much normal sexual activity on campuses today—and anyone over 40 who opens their eyes will be enlightened.

Why Antioch?

It is not by chance that Antioch College created this policy and that the reaction of the media has focused on this small campus. Antioch students have been free spirits for many decades and the campus governance system, which invests students with enormous responsibility in the decision-making process, enhances the likelihood that student issues will not only be talked about but acted upon. For years, Antioch students have been bringing to the campus cutting edge issues for their generation—whether from their high school or from their work experiences around the country that they alternate with on campus studies every three months. Now in the 1990s this open sexual environment has created a new wave of freedom dealing with consensual sexual relationships.

The development of the Antioch policy in the fall of 1990 was prompted by students' need to face the realities of the 1990s, and the feelings they have about their right to choose how and when to use their bodies. The policy deals with the creation of community standards to avoid the pain of date rape and unhappy sexual encounters in an environment in which sexual activity is common and easily accepted. And it focuses on standards of healthy interaction, not the policing of people.

Most surprising to many people is that Antioch students initiated the development of this policy and were critical players in each step of its creation and revision. It is clear to me that if this were not a student developed policy it would not have been accepted by the students. And it is widely accepted at Antioch College.

Personal reflection and the role of university leaders

But, while the students developed the policy, many adult, non-student members of the Antioch community actively participated in its development, especially the members of the College's executive council. As the Chair of that group, the Administrative Council (AdCil), it often fell to me to articulate the policy as it was being developed and to work with a number of critical students and faculty in bridging the huge differences of opinion. It fell to me, a "straight white man" in "power," to convince angry women students, a number of whom were not fond of men in general, especially those in powerful positions, that not only were we going to follow the democratic procedures of AdCil, but we were also going to follow the laws of the State of Ohio. The University's attorneys sat at the table and gave the students a short course on the fairness doctrine.

We all struggled to separate the real substantive issues from the anger and the attempted intimidation. All of the faculty and administrators on AdCil, who represented 8 of the 11 members (students represent the other 3), thought deeply about the pain being expressed by the students and the need to be fair to both the accused and the accuser. All of the non-students struggled with the explicitness of the language.

Now we had a policy that truly focused on healthy human relationships and not on policing prohibited behavior.

For me, especially, the sexual explicitness was difficult; not because of any prudishness—nobody has ever accused me of that—but because it fell to me as Chair of AdCil to voice publicly paragraph by paragraph the sexually explicit language. While there were no words in the policy that I had not heard or read, to read them in a serious way in public week after week taxed even my very high levels of tolerance for embarrassment.

I spent a good deal of time talking to my 21-year-old daughter, who was a student on campus. My daughter and I had agreed that we would not talk about campus matters, and we almost never violated that agreement. But on this issue we did talk. She was clearly heterosexual and had a good number of male friends. We discussed some of her sexual relationships openly and I learned a great deal about the life of students.

I learned that the policy was important, but I couldn't help seeing the pain it could cause. But, then, I also saw the pain that not having a policy could cause.

I thought long and hard about the issues of the fairness, about whether we were developing a good policy—which I believe happened—or being politically expedient in the context of very strong and strident student voices. I thought then and now about the charge of "male bashing." Was all of this male bashing, women getting even, or was it that life was no longer as comfortable for male students as it has always been? One woman Antioch Trustee may have summed it up when she said that the men may be experiencing what she as a woman had always experienced in college: that life wasn't always easy, that she had to watch out for herself, and that she wasn't always comfortable. I agree with her. Antioch College is no longer a male-dominant environment where men feel free to do whatever they choose. But, it is also not a female-dominant campus.

I also thought long and hard about the meaning of university leadership in the 1990s. The paradoxes for campus leaders in dealing with student sexual behavior are ever-present:

- we can't legislate student sexual behavior, but we must forge a policy regarding student sexual behavior;
- we must provide the leadership to make sure that a policy is developed, but we must be sure that it is articulated by students;
- we must talk with student leaders and especially women with a strong interest in these issues, yet the most active, and probably most knowledgeable, students and faculty are most suspicious of the motives of leaders;
- we must develop a policy in an open process in which students and interested faculty are directly involved, yet dealing with these volatile issues—like date rape—could expose the institution to neg-

ative publicity regarding events that were previously hidden, un-
addressed or even unknown;
- we must collaborate on the development of a policy that will create positive community expectations about healthy sexual behavior, yet we will be inundated with deeply disturbing examples of
  the breakdown of healthy sexual relationships and the need to include protection against sexual abuse.

Leadership in this area is difficult and painful because of what we
learn about the depths of experiences and pain of our students and because of the way we are treated. Even the most well meaning leader will
be treated with barely disguised hostility; the student advocates will assume that the president and other administrators represent the "tyranny
of silence" that has surrounded sexual abuse on university campuses.
Some of these students will become so intensely emotional they say
things they would later regret and probably forget, even though it will be
difficult for me to erase it from my mind. As symbols or live people, university leaders have to struggle with being perceived as part of the problem until a viable solution is developed.

It is also extremely sensitive work because we are working on the edge
of what we understand as older adults and in areas that have been off limits to institutional policies for over three decades. And, while I may be a
university leader, I am a human being who shares some of the taboos
about sexual matters and about intervening into this area of student life.

The sexual consent part of the policy, which emerged after six
months of revisions to the original policy, brought a sense of relief to
many of us—now we had a policy that truly focused on healthy human
relationships and not on policing prohibited behavior; it focused on educating students about standards of behavior, not on acting like a government agency.

But, I must admit that the process of developing this policy was gru-
eling work. In its entirety, it took place in two phases over a 14-month
period. It was personally the most painful process I've experienced in my
19 years as a chancellor and president of two universities. And, given my
experiences, that says a lot.

3

A Positive View
of the Antioch Plan

Eric Fassin

Eric Fassin is assistant director of the Institute of French Studies at New York University.

The so-called Antioch rules requiring students at Antioch College to obtain verbal consent before initiating any sexual act have been the subject of much controversy both within and without the academic community. Whether one is for or against the rules per se and their implicit and explicit consequences, one thing can be argued: The Antioch rules help clarify the understanding that sexuality is clearly a part of, not apart from, that human compact philosophers refer to as the social contract.

A good consensus is hard to find—especially on sexual politics. But the infamous rules instituted in 1992 by Antioch College which require students to obtain explicit verbal consent before so much as a kiss is exchanged, have created just that. They have provoked indignation (this is a serious threat to individual freedom!) as well as ridicule (can this be serious?). Sexual correctness thus proves a worthy successor to political correctness as a target in public debate.

Yet this consensus against the rules reveals shared assumptions among liberals, conservatives and even radicals about the nature of sex in our culture.

The new definition of consent at Antioch is based on a liberal premise: it assumes that sexual partners are free agents and that they mean what they say—yes means yes, and no means no. But the initiator must now obtain prior consent, step by step, which in practice shifts the burden of clarification from the woman to the man. The question is no longer "Did she say no?" but "Did she say yes?" Silence does not indicate consent, and it becomes his responsibility to dispel any ambiguity.

The novelty of the rules, however, is not as great as it seems. Antioch will not exert more control over its students; there are no sexual police. In practice, you still do what you want—as long as your partner does not complain . . . the morning after. If this is censorship, it intervenes ex post facto, not a priori.

In fact, the "threat" to individual freedom for most critics is not the invasion of privacy through the imposition of sexual codes, but the very existence of rules. Hence the success of polemicists like Katie Roiphe or Camille Paglia, who argue that feminism in recent years has betrayed its origins by embracing old-style regulations, paradoxically choosing the rigid 1950s over the liberating 1960s. Their advice is simply to let women manage on their own, and individuals devise their own rules. This individualist critique of feminism finds resonance with liberals, but also, strangely, with conservatives, who belatedly discover the perils of regulating sexuality.

But sexual laissez-faire, with its own implicit set of rules, does not seem to have worked very well recently. Since the collapse of established social codes, people play the same game with different rules. If more women are complaining of sexual violence, while more men are worrying that their words and actions might be misconstrued, who benefits from the absence of regulation?

A laissez-faire philosophy toward relationships assumes that sexuality is a game that can (and must) be played without rules, or rather that the invention of rules should be left to individual spontaneity and creativity, despite rising evidence that a rule of one's own often leads to misunderstandings. When acted out, individual fantasy always plays within preordained social rules. These rules conflict with the assumption in this culture that sex is subject to the reign of nature, not artifice, that it is the province of the individual, not of society.

> *The only question about the Antioch rules is not really whether we like them, but whether they improve the situation between men and women.*

Those who believe that society's constraints should have nothing to do with sex also agree that sex should not be bound by the social conventions of language. Indeed, this rebellion against the idea of social constraints probably accounts for the controversy over explicit verbal consent—from George Will, deriding "sex amidst semicolons," to Camille Paglia railing "As if sex occurs in the verbal realm." As if sexuality were incompatible with words. As if the only language of sex were silence. For *The New Yorker*, "the [Antioch] rules don't get rid of the problem of unwanted sex at all; they just shift the advantage from the muscle-bound frat boy to the honey-tongued French major."

This is not very different from the radical feminist position, which holds that verbal persuasion is no better than physical coercion. In this view, sexuality cannot be entrusted to rhetoric. The seduction of words is inherently violent, and seduction itself is an object of suspicion. (If this is true Marvell's invitation "To His Coy Mistress" is indeed a form of sexual harassment, as some campus feminists have claimed.)

What the consensus against the Antioch rules betrays is a common vision of sexuality which crosses the lines dividing conservatives, liberals and radicals. So many of the arguments start from a conventional situation, perceived and presented as natural: a heterosexual encounter with the man as the initiator, and the woman as gatekeeper—hence the focus on consent.

The outcry largely results from the fact that the rules undermine this traditional erotic model. Not so much by proscribing (legally), but by prescribing (socially). The new model, in which language becomes a normal form of erotic communication, underlines the conventional nature of the old one.

By encouraging women out of their "natural" reserve, these rules point to a new definition of sexual roles. "Yes" could be more than a way to make explicit the absence of a "no"; "yes" can also be a cry of desire. Women may express demands, and not only grant favors. If the legal "yes" opened the ground for an erotic "yes," if the contract gave way to desire and if consent led to demand, we would indeed enter a brave new erotic world.

New rules are like new shoes: they hurt a little at first, but they may fit tomorrow. The only question about the Antioch rules is not really whether we like them, but whether they improve the situation between men and women. All rules are artificial, but, in the absence of generally agreed-upon social conventions, any new prescription must feel artificial. And isn't regulation needed precisely when there is an absence of cultural consensus?

Whether we support or oppose the Antioch rules, at least they force us to acknowledge that the choice is not between regulation and freedom, but between different sets of rules, implicit or explicit. They help dispel the illusion that sexuality is a state of nature individuals must experience outside the social contract, and that eroticism cannot exist within the conventions of language. As Antioch reminds us, there is more in eroticism and sexuality than is dreamt of in this culture.

4

A Negative View
of the Antioch Plan

Pepper Schwartz

Pepper Schwartz is a professor of sociology at the University of Washington in Seattle.

The Antioch Plan, one of numerous such plans currently being promulgated throughout the country, attempts to govern sexual conduct. The problem with the Antioch model, and others of its kind, is that it ignores the multifaceted and contradictory nature of human sexuality. Since sexuality is different for different people, rules that may work for one group of persons can prove counterproductive, unfair, and even dangerous for another group.

Men and women today are grappling with the politics of yes. What does a solid yes look like? Who gets to say it, under what conditions, and how does it look different from no? After centuries of women's being denied the ability to say no, or to have consent-related issues taken seriously, supporters have been able to make the point that any kind of no should be an unambiguous stop. However, there has been less success at defining yes. Especially in the hot and heavy climate of maybe.

The debate has focused recently on rape, especially acquaintance rape. Some feminists—and I use the term broadly—furious at past and present egregious assaults that were never recognized as such or responded to adequately, have organized around this issue. The following concepts lie at the core of their argument:
* Male definitions of consent are inadequate.
* Male sexuality is fundamentally different from female sexuality.
* Male sexuality is dangerous.
* New personal and community standards need to be created and upheld in order to protect women.

Much of this seems mildly unarguable. We have a lot of research on misunderstandings and miscommunication of sexual intention between men and women. We certainly know that both the conscious and the unconscious misconstruing of a woman's right to say no exists. We also know that there are differences in male and female sexual socialization and that for reasons of sociology, and perhaps biology, an aroused and angry male can become aggressive and violent. No one who has studied sexual politics and sexuality would oppose better protections for women, better understanding by individuals of their own sexuality and that of others, and meaningful laws and punishments for those who viciously foist their sexual agendas on others.

But what has happened has gone well beyond all of that, and well beyond our understanding of human sexuality at this point in time. In fact, what is being offered as a viable restructuring of desire is in utter contradiction to what we know about how people have intercourse, how they want to have intercourse, and how they feel about what they are doing when they are having intercourse.

The new, politically correct version of sexuality is predicated upon four major untruths. The first is that human behavior is a clear-cut, sanitized entity. In life under the first myth, when people say no—or yes—they always mean it; people always know how they feel and never change or revise their interpretation of events after the fact.

In the second myth, male sexuality is exaggerated and demonized. It is certainly true that the vast majority of sexual crimes are committed by men, but overall, how many men commit such crimes? Male desire characterized by sexuality researchers as violent and voracious hardly fits the garden-variety teenage or adult male.

On the other hand, the third myth oversimplifies female sexuality by describing it as more passive, more consistent, more honest, and more generic than we know it to be. The women who are popping up in research papers on acquaintance rape and harassment are infantilized, devolved to permanently traumatized status, unable to function competently enough to say no, and unable to resist pressure from a boss or coworker.

The fourth myth posits that human sexuality is a homogenized, Barbie-and-Ken type of arrangement that is suitable for, desirable to, and practiced by a majority of men and women. Differentiation by culture, race, family background, dating experience, assorted personal characteristics, and a multitude of other factors is completely ignored.

The Antioch Plan

Let's take a closer look at this ideological caricature of sexuality by examining the Antioch University Plan, a set of campus rules developed by a group of undergraduate women to help extinguish unwanted sexual attentions and sexual miscommunication. In a letter published in November 1993 in the *Seattle Times*, Elizabeth Sullivan and Gabriel Metcalf, two proponents of the Antioch Plan, stated that the policy will accomplish the following:

- Remove the "gray area" between consent and coercion.
- Give a system of support for those who have experienced harassment or rape. Students called "peer advocates" will provide education and counseling for fellow students.
- Require that in any specific sexual encounter, each "escalating sexual act" be preceded by explicit verbal permission; otherwise rape is in progress. To quote the advocates, "this makes casual sex less likely because the door is closed to sex without verbal communication. Sexual scripts where those involved 'just know' that the person they are with wants them is disallowed by policy."

- Create a policy of "collective accountability" in which those who are "violated" can seek recourse. Sexual equality will be created because "the playing field will be leveled." Sexuality will be "controlled by culture as much as by one's sexual urges."

This is a system designed by women with a specific sense of what sexuality should be like—one that is rather reminiscent, at least superficially, of the 1950s.

Interestingly, the system is not explicitly gender-specific. Theoretically, either a women or a man could be doing the asking; however, there is no doubt that this is a system based on a model of aggressive male sexuality that the system's creators believe needs to be controlled.

In reality, for both men and women, this deconstruction of "escalating sex" would mean the imposition of a sexual style that neither would recognize—a sexual style requiring skills that are in relatively low supply among persons of both genders.

This system has already been widely attacked and satirized in the mass media. In her book entitled *The Morning After: Sex, Fear, and Feminism on Campus*, Katie Roiphe calls it "rape crisis feminism."[1] She is angered by the image of the passivity of women conjured up by this and similar proposals that assume the women have no ability to protect themselves from sexual aggression by acquaintances. Journalist George Will—someone I wouldn't normally cite—has written a scathing critique of what he believes is the Antioch Plan's assault on personal freedom. He refers to it as the legislation of "sexual style by committee."

Social agenda vs. social realities

My criticism of the Antioch Plan, and protocols like it, is that these rules do not fit with existing data and fail to address the complex nature of human sexuality. They contradict sexual reality just as much as the virginity cults of the 1950s, the strict notions of Victorian womanhood and rapacious male sexuality at the turn of the century, or the claim in China during the Cultural Revolution that there was no homosexuality in that country. Those constructions never fit the data; this one is no exception.

This is not to deny that each society tries to socially construct sexuality—and to some extent succeeds. However, it is the role of sexuality researchers to expose these attempts for what they are, and to study and write about what people really do, social constructions and efforts at social control aside. It is critical to understand and recognize how people actually behave, and to question and critique policies created in violation of these realities.

Sexuality is messy, passionate, unclear, tentative, anxiety-producing, liberating, frightening, embarrassing, consoling, appetitive, and cerebral. In other words, sexuality is contradictory, it is different for different people, and it is even different for the same person at different times. Sexuality operates at three or four levels at once.

We study human sexuality and know its range. We know that each society makes rules about what constitutes healthy or allowable sexuality and that these rules match the social purposes of the culture. But what are the social purposes of our society at this moment in time? And how do they match what we know about what we study?

For the purpose of discussion, let us divide sexuality between men and women into two categories. The first group will contain well-meaning, if inept, sexual seekers and lovers. The second will contain narcissists who are incapable of taking another person's feelings or rights into account. These are users, persons who are fearful, aggressive, angry, potentially dangerous, and occasionally lethal.

We know a lot about both groups. The seekers and lovers include most people, and they are rarely state-of-the-art sexual experts. They have fears and act compulsively; their behavior is hormonally and culturally scripted. They generally feel inadequate; many need strong interpersonal encouragement or chemical courage to proceed. They are generally poor communicators, both with themselves and with others. And they are inconsistent when it comes to basic health precautions—few use condoms regularly or as the situation warrants. When they have sex, even with a steady partner, they are often ill at ease with their body and with certain behaviors or positions. They turn the lights out. They want to be loved or they want to get it over with—sometimes both. While our research is less complete on the most successful among them, the data suggest that the confident, self-assured, uninhibited, unrepressed, good communicator, good listener is the smaller part of their ranks. In *Constructing the Sexual Crucible,*[2] David Schnarch tells that intimacy is so hard for most people, even long-term married couples have trouble looking deeply into each other's eyes during intercourse.

> *My criticism of the Antioch Plan, and protocols like it, is that these rules do not fit with existing data and fail to address the complex nature of human sexuality.*

As scary as sex may be, however, most men and women desire and seek it. Nervous or not, the yearning for intimacy or pleasure sends them, sometimes at a very young age, in search of physical connection with someone else.

The second group of people are the ones we think of when we make rules about stranger and acquaintance rape. Unfortunately, since these individuals think only of themselves or are sociopathic in other ways, since they are insecure and often angry, perhaps sadistic, they are the least likely to listen to or observe a nicely laid out set of rules, or even to consider that those rules apply to them. They are also the least likely to understand when they have broken the rules, or to recognize that there should be consequences for doing so. They are people incapable of empathizing with and respecting the needs of others.

The problem with the Antioch University model and others of its kind that are worming their way into educational, workplace, and social environments is that they analyze this second group's sexuality and use it to make rules for the first. They remake sexuality according to a vision of female vulnerability that does not take into account either the biology of arousal or the desires of the full continuum of men or women. What they offer are rules that are ineffective, dangerous, and inapplicable to those honestly looking for direction. Their vision demonizes male sexuality, civilizes ordinary sex out of existence, and applies a jerry-rigged sexual structure to well-meaning folks fumbling along in desire and fear.

Is the situation so precarious, are rape and molestation and harassment so much the fabric of male sexuality, that we need Antioch-like protection? Do we really need the types of sexual harassment laws where a hand on the shoulder can precede a report to the ombudsperson or an attorney? Do we as sexuality researchers see the world as so sexually oppressive, volatile, and threatening that all unwanted or inappropriate sexual behavior needs to be controlled through formal procedures? Is this really the sexual behavior we see in everyday life?

The vagaries of desire

And then there is the larger question: Can we really sort behaviors into discrete meanings without gray areas? Granted, sexuality is reasonably malleable. It is probably possible to "train" men and women to hesitate at every turn, check each emotion, and never touch another human being without spoken permission—but does that mean we should? Does our research tell us this is what people want and need? Is this in any way congruent with species behaviors? What is our role as researchers? What truths do our data tell us, or more to the point, which truths do we miss if we become ideological, narrow in focus, and wrapped up in the purposes of a prevailing ideology, however noble its intent?

I have studied homosexuality, bisexuality, and female sexuality for some of the same reasons others have studied rape or other controversial topics. The work I have read has not always fit my intuitions or the behavior I have observed. I have seen unanswered questions. I have observed social injustices that seemed to be based on faulty data. I have wanted to answer these neglected questions and illuminate both colleagues and the public at large

Sexuality, in all its forms, has always fascinated me. Our maleness and femaleness come from so many complex sources; we are creatures of culture as well as of DNA. How we love and desire, and where these desires come from are not easy questions to answer; they are deep enough to spend a lifetime in discovery.

Today, our society is at war with itself on what desire is permissible and worthy. There is a party line by sex, by circumstance, by intensity, by frequency—how much is just right, how much is deficient? When is more not enough, when is it too much? We should be careful to avoid the trap of "setting a schedule" of appropriate sexual conduct as if sexuality were a mathematically generated paint-by-numbers puzzle. Clearly, we can agree that no one should be forced to have sex against his or her will. But even will is a confused, disorderly entity. Who among us has not had strong, conflicting feelings, desire and ambivalence—a yes that should have been a no, a no that should have been a yes. Certainly there are cases of absolute clarity; there are also cases of uncertainty, confusion, and vacillation.

The role of researchers

Our society imposes a social meaning upon every kind of desire; we disallow it in children; we satirize and patronize it in the very old. We have seen great changes in the politics of desire over the last few decades, and will surely see more. The question is where we, as researchers, will be in the provision of data, wisdom, and analysis on these topics.

We must be able to look at the data and not pretend morality is science, or at least to know when we are blending the two. When we call someone compulsive, let us at least acknowledge that this is a human trait, widely dispersed among our species. We have the natural capacity to overeat, overwork, overworry, overexercise, overeverything. Is something so firmly embedded in our species abnormal, or is this just one outlet for a common trait that expresses itself in numerous ways—and that may be dangerous only in certain situations or in extreme cases?

If behavioral science is going to survive the shifting scenario of the politics of desire, we must be mindful of the following points:

- We should acknowledge whatever the biology is and do our research within it. For example, we might be able to construct a society with no homosexual acts in it, but we could not construct one without homosexual desire; let us acknowledge those facts.
- We must understand the social constructs of our times and acknowledge how they shape our understanding of desire, as well as how these lenses affect the way we look at data and what we find.
- We need to avoid presumptions, so that we can resist folding into the common wisdom. Our goal is to preserve our role as investigators, lest we dishonor our training by becoming unconscious agents of social control. As researchers, it is our job to add light; there will always be others who can add heat.

Notes

1. Roiphe, K. *The Morning After: Sex, Fear, and Feminism on Campus* (Boston: Little, Brown, and Co., 1993).

2. Schnarch, D.M. *Constructing the Sexual Crucible* (New York: W.W. Norton and Co., 1991).

An Alternative Plan
to Control Campus Rape

Carol Bohmer and Andrea Parrot

Carol Bohmer is a lawyer and an associate professor in the Graduate School of Public and International Affairs at the University of Pittsburgh. Andrea Parrot is an assistant professor in the Department of Human Service Studies at Cornell University in Ithaca, New York. She is cofounder and chair of the Cornell Coalition Advocating Rape Education.

Prevention programs are the best solution for reducing the number of rapes on campus. However, since even the best prevention programs will not eliminate campus rape, effective policies dealing with rapes that have occurred also must be available. To be effective, these policies should be of a nature that victims will not be reticent to report assaults and more important, should convince potential assailants that punishment will be sure and swift. Suggestions for policies, procedures, and educational efforts to prevent and to deal with rape on campus are presented.

Although educational programs will not guarantee that acquaintance rape and sexual assault will stop, they may help in reducing the number of sexual assaults on a campus. In addition, if a college is making an effort to prevent rape through educational and other programs, it is less likely to be sued successfully in civil court.

The best way to deal with sexual assault on campus is to prevent it, so colleges should make sure that they have comprehensive rape prevention programs available to all of their students; programs for men are of special importance. In addition, any member of the campus professional or student community who is likely to interact with victims and assailants should have training in how to deal with these issues (for example, medical personnel, residence life staff, and campus police). No matter how good the rape prevention efforts are on campus, however, it is unlikely that rape will be eliminated completely. Therefore, effective policies and procedures must be in place to deal with rapes that do occur. If a case is reported, the victim must receive support, and if the allegations are proven, the assailant should be dealt with to the fullest extent that campus policy permits. This will give the message to others who would

Reprinted with the permission of Lexington Books, an imprint of The Free Press, a Division of Simon & Schuster, from *Sexual Assault on Campus* by Carol Bohmer and Andrew Parrot. Copyright ©1993 by Lexington Books.

commit a similar act that such behavior is not acceptable.

Victims are not likely even to report a rape to the campus police if the judicial process on campus is poorly run. Most victims of acquaintance rape and sexual assault do not attempt to have the assailant arrested; they would like him to know that what he did was wrong, however, so that he will not repeat that type of behavior with others. Even more importantly, victims want and need emotional help so that they can put the assault behind them and get on with their lives. For some victims, going to the police adds to their emotional trauma rather than reducing it, so they often choose to talk to someone at the counseling center (or a sympathetic friend) rather than to the police.

If the college institutes the suggestions offered here, more women will probably come forward as victims, not only to press charges but to utilize the counseling services available to them. Fewer men will consider it acceptable to take advantage of women sexually. Colleges will be better places for students to study, learn, and develop into well-rounded adults. Once an effective rape prevention program is implemented and campus policies and procedures are tightened up, the reporting rate of rape will probably increase in the short run. Once the word is out to students that rape will not be tolerated on campus (and offenders are separated from campus), however, the rate of rape should decrease. Of course, because defendants are considered innocent until proven guilty, colleges must be careful to protect their rights as well. Unfortunately, though, colleges have historically been much better at providing the defendant with his rights than the victim with hers.

> *Implementation and enforcement of effective policies are probably the most important element in reducing the incidence of sexual assault on campus.*

It is possible to change the way acquaintance rapes are handled on college campuses. Although policy recommendations are the most important first step, there are many other avenues administrators can pursue to make campuses safer. All members of the college community will benefit from decreasing the number of acquaintance rapes on campus. Funds should be allocated to carry out all of the policy, procedural, and educational recommendations listed below. In addition, research should be funded to determine the acquaintance rape patterns on campus—where it happens, how often, and under what circumstances. Prevention efforts are most effective if they are aimed at the specified patterns and problems on a given campus. This money will be well spent; it will save the college from spending money defending lawsuits, and from losing contributions or applicants as a result of bad publicity about mismanaged cases.

Implementation and enforcement of effective policies are probably the most important element in reducing the incidence of sexual assault on campus. Once students realize that they will not be able to get away with committing sexual assault on campus, they are likely to stop. Publicity about suspensions and expulsions for that type of offense will serve as a deterrent for others. Educational programs are also necessary so that all students, faculty, and staff know what acquaintance rape is, that it will not be tolerated on campus, how to proceed if it occurs, and what they can expect if acquaintance rape does occur. Judicial policies and procedures that condemn acquaintance rape and carry harsh sanctions are important to send a message to all potential rapists that they will be severely punished if they are found guilty of committing an acquaintance rape on campus. The summary of recommendations that follows provides specific suggestions to carry out these aims.

Recommendations to create a campus free of acquaintance rape

I. Administrative policies and procedures
    A. Administrative response
        1. Administration must take a tough stand with assailants
        2. Eliminate or reevaluate the role of organizations that commit or support gang or acquaintance rape
        3. Carefully examine the fraternity system and structure, and revise if necessary
        4. The first violation of the policy should be dealt with swiftly and harshly; even if the case does not result in a criminal conviction the college policy should be carried out
        5. Establish a position on campus for someone to train safety officers and counselors, confer with university counsel, monitor these cases, and support those involved in such cases
        6. Create a rapid response team to be mobilized in the event of a reported rape
        7. Provide proactive and preventive (rather than reactive) media coverage
        8. Conduct research to determine the extent of the problem on your campus, and develop programs and interventions to reflect its needs
        9. Develop and implement a third-party reporting mechanism
    B. Personnel recommendations
        1. Coordination with local police agencies
        2. Some mechanism to collect and disseminate accurate statistics
        3. Implementation of security measures to reduce the likelihood of acquaintance sexual assault victimization
        4. Organize a task force or coalition representing the following:
            a. Dean of students' office
            b. Residence life
            c. Public safety
            d. Health center
                (1) Health education department
                (2) Psychological services
                (3) Sex counselor
                (4) Medical personnel
            e. Academic faculty
                (1) Women's studies
                (2) Psychology
                (3) Sociology
                (4) Human development and family studies
                (5) Nursing
                (6) Political science
                (7) Philosophy

            (8) Criminal justice
            (9) Law
           (10) Social work
           (11) Human service studies
           (12) Medicine
           (13) Physical education
           (14) Health education
      f. Local rape crisis center
      g. Religious organizations on campus
      h. Office of equal opportunity
      i. Students
      j. Intrafraternity council
      k. Pan-Hellenic council
      1. International students office

C. Personnel safety recommendations
   1. Public safety
      a. "Blue light" direct phones to public safety throughout campus
      b. Special free buses after dark with stops at "blue light" phones
      c. Escort service at night
      d. Special training for safety officers
   2. Safe houses

D. Financial
   1. Allocate funds for prevention of sexual assault
   2. Support research to determine the extent of the problem on your campus

E. Policy
   1. Develop a college policy regarding acceptable sexual behavior (similar to those for alcohol and drugs); the policy should clearly outline penalties that will follow specific behaviors
   2. Establish a written protocol for dealing with sexual assault cases (available in a sexual assault intervention handbook), including the following:
      a. College policy regarding sexual assault on campus
      b. Notification procedures and designated personnel to be notified (with victim consent)
      c. Legal reporting requirements and procedures
      d. Services available for victims
      e. On- and off-campus resources available
      f. Procedures for ongoing case management
      g. Procedures for guaranteeing confidentiality
      h. Minimum mandatory sentences
      i. Prohibiting graduation while charges are pending against the accused
      j. Preventing registration for future semesters until the condition of the sentence has been satisfied
      k. The accused may be moved from his residence hall at the discretion of the victim
   3. Judicial code recommendations
      a. Visitors to campus who are sexually assaulted on campus should be covered under the policy
      b. Sanctions may be applied against organizations that condone rape or sexual assault

      c. Terms such as *lack of consent, rape* and *sexual assault* should be clearly defined in the campus code of conduct

  4. Hearing recommendations
      a. Closed hearings should always be provided as an option
      b. Rape shield laws should apply
      c. Witnesses should be made known to both sides seventy-two hours before the hearing
      d. Allow the victim's testimony to be videotaped in appropriate circumstances
      e. Develop a written agreement with the District Attorney at a campus hearing that will not violate the defendant's Fifth Amendment rights
      f. Accord defendants and victims the same rights

  5. Defendant's rights
      a. To be treated as innocent until proven guilty
      b. A rapid hearing, if possible
      c. Respect
      d. To minimize as much as possible the length of time he is suspended prior to the hearing
      e. To be informed, in writing, of the charges against him
      f. To be given written notice of the hearing at least two days in advance
      g. To receive a list of witnesses who will appear in support of the charges
      h. Veto power over any judicial board members
      i. To bring an advisor
      j. To remain silent
      k. To examine witnesses and documentary evidence, and to provide an explanation and argument on his behalf
      l. To receive, upon request, a written transcript or tape of the proceedings
      m. To appeal the decision

  6. Victim's rights
      a. To decide whether to press charges
      b. To have an advisor present at the hearing
      c. To have living arrangements modified, if necessary
      d. To be present at the hearing
      e. Not to have sexual history discussed during the hearing
      f. To be notified immediately of the outcome of the hearing
      g. To be separated from the defendant during the hearing, by a screen, closed circuit TV, or by means of tape recordings
      h. To be present during the hearing
      i. To have counsel or adviser available during the hearing

F. Services for victims
  1. Provide the victim with as much support as she needs, but do not pressure her to pursue a course of action with which she is uncomfortable; if she wants to press charges, help her with that process, but respect her wishes if she does not want to pursue legal recourse
  2. Establish a comprehensive program for assisting victims
  3. Referral to free therapists trained in acquaintance rape
  4. Availability of a trained victim advocate

  5. Counseling
     a. Individual counseling
     b. Acquaintance rape victim support groups
     c. Support groups for significant others
     d. Victim's assistance advocates
  6. Trained medical personnel available to provide care for the victim and to collect evidence if necessary
II. Educational efforts
  A. Training for faculty and staff
     1. Train support staff (residence life, counselors, public safety, etc.) to deal with this problem
     2. Train medical personnel to examine and provide services to acquaintance rape victims
     3. Encourage faculty to discuss this issue in their classes
  B. Provide programs for all students on acquaintance rape and strategies
     1. Discuss acquaintance rape in orientation programs for new students
     2. Provide programs in single-sex living units, such as residence halls, fraternities, and sororities
     3. Make women's self-defense classes available
     4. Offer assertiveness training for males and females
     5. Provide self-esteem programs for males and females
     6. Offer programs on the dysfunction of sex-role stereotyping
     7. Develop programs for all-male groups prone to this type of behavior
     8. Hold a special orientation session each semester with international students to describe appropriate behavior towards women on campus
     9. Make the sexual assault policy known to all students during new student orientation in an oral and written presentation
     10. Contact parents before and while their children are your students
  C. Programs should reflect administration philosophy regarding acquaintance rape issues
     1. Address these programs to men as well as women
     2. Inform students that they may be civilly as well as legally liable for psychological and physical injuries resulting from harassment or acquaintance rape
     3. Involve fraternities and sororities in the planning and implementation of programs
     4. Involve the student government in funding, sponsorship, and/or implementation of rape education programs
     5. Appeal directly to male campus leaders, fraternity presidents, and sports team captains to get involved; they may be able to influence others
     6. Ensure that there is a mechanism to coordinate all these prevention efforts
  D. Written materials should be developed and disseminated
     1. Develop and provide an informal brochure for all students explaining what victims should do
     2. Admissions literature should address the problem and state

that the campus administration is committed to preventing and prosecuting acquaintance rape

E. Information should be delivered in a variety of traditional and nontraditional ways
1. Utilize alternate information and delivery programs
    a. Printed media
    b. Computer-accessible information
    c. Nonprinted media
2. Create a speakers bureau of interested faculty, students, and staff and train them appropriately; provide presenters with an honorarium
3. Organize a campus wide "speak out" to sensitize the campus community
4. Offer a program of a "mock trial" of an acquaintance rape
5. Have representatives from the local women's center provide programs or assistance in planning programs
6. Post announcements of programs in male living quarters, locker rooms, etc.
7. Males should cofacilitate programs on acquaintance rape
8. Develop a master list of all resources and programs available relating to acquaintance rape programs (for the use of counselors, health professionals, students, and researchers)
9. Publicize incidence date regarding acquaintance rapes and penalties in the campus newspaper
10. Use campus radio and TV to make public service announcements
11. Exposure to this information should be repetitive and varied in presentation
12. The terms sexual assault, acquaintance rape, date rape, etc., should not be in the title; those terms will scare away those who need to hear the message the most
13. Use theater (both improvisational and plays) to raise consciousness on campus
14. Hold a "take back the night" march
15. Have a "rape education" week
16. Cancel classes one day and hold rape awareness events
17. Publicize a "myth of the month" in the school paper or on bookmarks

F. Alcohol-related efforts
1. Provide interesting nonalcoholic events for students
2. Discourage the consumption of alcohol by students
3. Enforce the college's alcohol policy; do not permit drinking in rooms if students are underage
4. The first time a student violates the campus code while drinking, mandate participation in an alcohol program and impose probation
5. Realize that campus sexual assaults are almost always alcohol related

6

Sexual Politics on Campus:
A Case Study

Philip Weiss

Philip Weiss is a contributing editor of Harper's Magazine.

When a female student at Dartmouth College who was allegedly assaulted by a male student later learned of another, similar accusation against the same student, she pressed charges, but the male student was found not guilty. Then a third female student, learning of the charges against the accused, decided to press charges for an alleged assault on her by the same male two and a half years earlier. This time the male student was found guilty of abuse; he was suspended for one term, a decision the state courts subsequently refused to overturn. The handling of these successive cases against the male student illustrates a changing attitude on college campuses, one that exhibits a new sensitivity to female charges of sexual abuse. But the male student was not granted such understanding: he became a symbol, a focus for the community's pent-up anger about past abuses and insensitivity, as accusing posters with his photo were posted and activists "picketed" him on campus.

Petite Jane Pfaff has a doelike poise I associate with pictures of campus life twenty-five years ago, and the self-conscious postures she and I have taken on the overstuffed furniture of Kappa Kappa Gamma's living room bring back the awkwardness of outdated courtship rituals. In her turtleneck sweater she's tentative and unreachable, while I feel big, clumsy, worried I'll say the wrong thing. Outside the white clapboard sorority house the Dartmouth College campus is about to begin its annual fall rites; freshmen are stacking heavy pine timbers on the Green for the bonfire on Friday night. Dartmouth men will dance around the blaze like their belovedly imagined Indians. They'll get drunk and naked and whoop the old college war cry, "Wah-Hoo-Wah." It's hard to forget that this is the campus that inspired *Animal House*.

But Jane Pfaff, whose sorority I'd come to visit because it is active in addressing sexual issues, would like us to forget that picture. She's holding out two letters—one signed by the Sigma Delta sorority and the other by Kappa Kappa Gamma's executive committee—the wording of which is anything but tentative:

"Amid recent rumors of alleged acts involving VOYEURISM, SEXUAL HARASSMENT and SEXUAL ASSAULT, we feel the need to express our outrage. We have been silent too long," reads the letter from Sigma Delta. "Witnesses to these crimes who have not come forward are equally responsible . . ." In one rumored incident to which the letter refers, a group of men had stood hunched outside a fraternity-house window as a brother made it with a drunken woman. Then the men had come into the bedroom and hovered over her body to watch; the woman had been too drunk to realize that the man was lying when he assured her they were alone.

Kappa Kappa Gamma's letter reads, "By breaking our silence and acknowledging the problem, we are ending our inadvertent acceptance of these atrocities."

There was a time, not very long ago, when fraternity voyeurism was regarded as a prank—distasteful, even morally repugnant, but a prank. Its characterization as an "atrocity" reflects the fact that, almost overnight, Dartmouth has become a village of concern over sexual issues. It was news of this unlikely transformation that brought me to Dartmouth, in Hanover, New Hampshire, last summer [1990] and again in the fall; I'd heard that, in the aftermath of a single, dramatic case, the school's familiar image as a scratching post for the animals of the Ivy League had given way to a regime of sensitivity.

> *Society seems at last prepared to recognize—on college campuses anyway—. . . the rape of women by men they know.*

On first impression, the revolution appeared complete. The council of fraternities and sororities had organized a Sexual Awareness Week. The right-wing *Dartmouth Review*, a bastion of unreconstructed male chauvinism, was suddenly decrying the tendency of Dartmouth men to treat women with "hostility . . . [as] herds of cattle." A group called REACT was going around campus giving a lecture-and-video presentation on "myths and stereotypes about rape." One night a man in the audience announced that he was taking down the *Playboy* pinup from his wall.

Similar scenes of awareness and conversion are taking place on campuses all over the country today. And with the issue of date rape on campus commanding the media's attention, society seems at last prepared to recognize—on college campuses anyway—a new category of sexual crime: the rape of women by men they know. At the same time, the campus activists who succeeded in bringing this overdue sensitivity to the subject of date rape are now pushing to gain recognition of new forms of offensive conduct, variously designated as "sexual abuse," "sexual coercion," and "sexual harassment," wide categories that sometimes seem to have less to do with a specific set of deeds committed by men than with certain feelings experienced by women.

These issues had arrived on the Dartmouth campus with great force. The college had endured a widely publicized case involving not rape but a related act, an alleged assault by an aggressive male against a passive female. It was termed a case of "sexual abuse." Eventually it found its way into court. Hundreds of pages of confidential disciplinary proceedings were made public. (The school seems to specialize in public dramas; this is the college that was in the news a few years ago for its students' sledge-hammer attacks on antiapartheid shanties on the Green and more recently for an uproar over a quote from Hitler that appeared on the mast-head of the *Review*.)

This time the party of sensitivity had won a resounding victory. "We want to be on the cutting edge of sexual-assault issues," Brian Ellner, the student assembly president, told me in October 1990. "This issue is one that our generation must confront." Today the dean's office is telling students that they should not have sex without a clearly stated "yes" on both sides. Sexual-abuse activists are holding workshops to help students recast the male psyche. Students are even questioning the appropriate-ness of the college bonfire, with its holocaust of waste, its incitements to male abandon.

His beloved college had suspended him for what a Dartmouth statement called "an encounter in a men's bathroom."

New mores are in force. Because of an episode that came to be known as the Acker case, sorority girls like Jane Pfaff have been transformed into sexual-abuse activists, and a college campus has been turned upside down.

It is a short walk from Kappa Kappa Gamma, along a slight hill—the incline of the Connecticut River valley—past the whitewashed adminis-tration buildings with their verdigris roofs, to Richardson Hall, the dor-mitory where the Acker case began more than three years ago, without anyone knowing it was beginning.

Richardson is a mishmash of oaken Ivy League prestige and adoles-cent romper room. Jammed up against the wide staircase on the first floor is a Ping-Pong table. Nearby is the bathroom—a "two-holer" in the rustic Dartmouth nomenclature: old marble stalls gone a little mossy and wooden doors hung by nickel fixtures. This bathroom, so central to the Acker case, is not open and clear with wide clean sightlines, as you might imagine it, but narrow and cramped.

It was a weekend night in October 1987. A group of drunken fresh-men was moving restlessly from a party in the basement of Topliff, a dorm, to a bigger party in another dorm, Mid-Mass, and stopped at Richardson to pick someone up. By sophomore year, the same students would be centering their social life around fraternities.

Among the group of freshmen was a woman I'll call Alma Lee,* a Ko-rean-American from the Midwest who had graduated from a New En-gland prep school. She's of medium height, athletically built, attractive, and from a conservative family that put a great deal of emphasis on achievement. Alma Lee is not what would be considered traditional Dart-

---

* Although "Alma Lee" has been identified by her actual name in the press on more than one occasion, I have chosen here to respect her desire for anonymity.

mouth material. Her presence in part reflects new president James O. Freedman's emphasis on diversity, on ending what he calls Dartmouth's "boys will be boys" culture.

Alma had drunk four or five beers, and she needed to pee. She went into the two-holer, which at the time was a men's room; there were no women's rooms in Richardson, the school having not yet completed the integration of its facilities fifteen years after first admitting women.

Another student from the group of freshmen was also in the men's room: Kevin Acker, a blunt man from Dallas whose thick build and dark curly hair give him a resemblance to Sluggo. Alma had noticed him going up to the women in the group, trying to sniff their necks, saying, "Mmmm, you smell good."

Much later there would be a dispute about who was in the bathroom first, Kevin Acker or Alma Lee, about who approached whom, about who led whom into one of the casket-size marble stalls. Three years later a lot about this night would be fuzzy and contentious. For instance, Acker would say that they were in the Richardson men's room for eight minutes; Alma would say it was three.

When the two came out of the bathroom and the group of '91s plunged back into the brisk air of the New Hampshire fall, Alma Lee's mood had changed, according to Craig Rush, a friend who was there. She didn't want to go on to Mid-Mass anymore; she asked Rush to walk her home. Later he'd recall how she held a little too tightly to his side, how she didn't say much. She asked him to wait at the door until someone else went in, until she knew she would not be alone inside. It seemed a bit odd to him, but he didn't make anything of this behavior for another three years.

A few weeks later, Alma's friend David Lillard learned part of what happened that night. He heard from Craig Rush that Acker had been boasting that he "scammed" with Alma Lee in the Richardson bathroom. When Lillard told Alma about the boast, she flared with anger—her third week at the school and she's "pinned" in a bathroom by a stranger.

"I . . . internalized it and tried to not think of it ever," she said later. As a result, it would be another two and a half years before she told her story and before Edward J. Shanahan, Dartmouth College dean, learned of a paradoxical idiom current among his students when he interrupted the testimony, in a closed hearing on the Alma Lee matter, to ask what Craig Rush meant by the word "scam."

"Scamming?" Rush said. "Scamming applies to a kind of physical contact . . . sexual contact."

Before [1989] at Dartmouth, the sexual landscape had been a treacherous one for women.

When I visited Dartmouth, I asked several students what they meant by scamming. It wasn't anything you'd do with your girlfriend or boyfriend, they said; it was more illicit than that and included everything from making out to intercourse. Sometimes it was very nearly random: the sorts of things that happen at the end of parties. It conveyed a mutuality of purpose, like "gamming," the word for meetings at sea. But I couldn't sever the word from its real-world meaning—of having conned someone—and perhaps in that association lay some of Alma Lee's pain.

The first time I saw Kevin Acker, August 28, 1990, he was steaming into a bathroom—this time with his lawyer—at the Grafton County Courthouse, outside the little town of North Haverhill, New Hampshire, in the foothills of the White Mountains thirty-five miles north of campus, during the first and only public hearing on his case. Everything Acker does seems to have a steaming, straight-ahead quality, a tapir's clumsy persistence. It was partly due to this quality that Acker had become something of a big man on campus in the three years that had passed since that night freshman year.

Now his beloved college had suspended him for what a Dartmouth statement called "an encounter in a men's bathroom," and Acker was suing the school to have the suspension lifted. Making his case to the judge, his tone was that of the BMOC who has suffered incomprehensible indignities: "I plan to apply for the Rhodes, Marshall, and Fulbright scholarships. It would prove difficult for me to prepare my applications well if I am not on campus," he said. "I've resigned as editor of *The Dartmouth* [the school daily]. I expect that my membership in Casque & Gauntlet [a society of student leaders] will be terminated. . . ."

Wearing a light tweed jacket, Acker flushed as he catalogued these disgraces for the judge. He had already stepped down from Palaeopitus, the senior society of twenty that, in fireside chats, advises the dean and president on affairs at the college.

"Allow me to . . . walk around this campus with my head held high," he'd pleaded with the college's disciplinary committee six weeks before this hearing. He had paid for a lie-detector test to show he was telling the truth when he answered no to the question, "Did Alma protest verbally or physically in any way when you touched her. . . ?"

School judicial boards are hard-pressed to sort out the facts of, say, a plagiarism case, let alone a rape.

Even Alma Lee had agreed, in confidential testimony two months earlier, that she hadn't said no. But Acker had been convicted of sexual abuse just the same. His conduct would have been regarded as unextraordinary, he testified in court, had the college not been overwhelmed by "radicals."

Dartmouth's lawyer asked if it wasn't true that students were supposed to get an explicit "yes" before proceeding with sex. Acker mocked him. "'Can I touch you here? Can I touch you here?' I think it would be viewed as extremely strange by females to require a 'yes, yes, yes,'" he said. "It certainly is not the standard observed by males on the Dartmouth campus." He bristled when he said that, and it was obvious just how much Acker had judged his own behavior by that of his peers.

In many ways Acker was an outsider in Hanover. A Jew, the son of a small businessman, he was one of President Freedman's recruits, part of the newly "diverse" Dartmouth. In contrast to the classic Dartmouth figure—the laid-back preppie with an athlete's cap turned the wrong way on his head—Acker took his work terribly seriously. An uncomfortable-seeming person, he had gained a reputation for abrasive arrogance. "He's widely despised," I was told by Hugo Restall, the executive editor of *The*

Dartmouth Review. Freshman year Acker was turned down by a fraternity, but he rushed again as a sophomore and got in.

By his junior year Acker had climbed to the higher reaches of Dartmouth society, becoming editor in chief of *The Dartmouth.* From his post there, the Dallas boy attacked both the campus radicals and the right-wingers on *The Review*, whose politics he shared but whose old-Dartmouth clubbiness put him off.

It was soon after Kevin Acker had achieved this prominence that things started to come apart for him.

Where it started

In retrospect, Kevin Acker's undoing can be dated to the day in 1989, during the fall of his junior year, when Heather Earle arrived in Hanover. The college had gone looking for a full-time, permanent sexual-awareness and sexual-harassment counselor, its first, and found the then twenty-six-year-old psychologist in Mankato, Minnesota. Such a transformative moment has taken place at many other schools in the past few years. Typically, the college comes to the realization that there is a problem with the sexual practices of young men and women living on the same halls, getting drunk at the same parties, and, often enough, going to bed with one another, sometimes with unhappy results. At one time this unhappiness might have been thought of as part of growing up, even as personal tragedy. The Heather Earles see it very differently—as a social problem and an injustice.

I met the counselor in her basement office in a building known as Dick's House, the campus health service. She reminded me of Mary Poppins—tall, kind, no-nonsense, and slightly censorious. She has tousled dark hair and a narrow face with lively, sensitive dark eyes. She wore flat shoes, a purplish dress, and a cardigan in a dull purple snowflake pattern. On the desk lay her beeper, which alerts her at all hours to the calls of victims of sexual abuse. She refers to these women as "survivors." "When you use the word 'victim,'" she explains, "you kind of picture a small, poor victim, [someone] that's continuously a victim."

Before Earle arrived at Dartmouth, the sexual landscape had been a treacherous one for women, particularly freshmen. Parietal rules governing the interaction between men and women on campus had long since fallen. Fraternity membership was high, drawing complaints similar to those being heard on campuses all over the country: that the frats lacked adequate supervision, that at basement parties members used alcohol to get women into bed. "There was enormous confusion . . . about what the courting expectations were and what the expectations of intimacy were on the part of both men and women," Dean Edward Shanahan told me. "Both men and women did not know how to behave amid that confusion. . . . There were abuses occurring within the community that somehow were not coming to the surface. . . . We were perhaps seeing the tip of the iceberg."

One reason women didn't come forward more often is that predominantly male administrations have been reluctant to deal with their complaints. There is, of course, the fear that bad publicity will cut down on already disappointing application figures. But there is also the fact that school judicial boards are hard-pressed to sort out the facts of, say, a plagiarism case, let alone a rape. Dartmouth's Committee on Standards, its disciplinary board, had dealt with several cases of what the Student Handbook called sexual abuse, but the closed proceedings had sent out confused signals. In a report of one case (which the college refuses to discuss), a football player was said to have been found guilty of forcing sexual intercourse on a woman, but his suspension, conveniently, did not keep him from returning to the gridiron the following fall.

Despite such apparent clumsiness on the part of the college, few at Dartmouth question that the administration is the proper arbiter of such disputes. To someone who was in college during the early Seventies, this is one of the surprising dimensions of sexual politics on campus today; the administration was the last place we looked to for redress of our grievances. But today's students do not want to sort out these issues among themselves. Nor do they want to go to the D.A. They're evidently comfortable with *in loco parentis*, the college's traditional power as substitute parent. On the post-Reagan college campus, the administration is viewed as a benevolent, if often negligent, father figure. An unspoken understanding exists that sexual abuse on campus is a problem not for society at large to solve but for the campus family, the not-yet-adult society of the school, with its own special code of behavior.

The psychologist told Dartmouth's women that their feelings of being violated by aggressive men deserved expression.

To this troubled family, Heather Earle brought a feminist healing touch. The psychologist told Dartmouth's women that their feelings of being violated by aggressive men deserved expression. She argued that when they suppress such pain it will only break out in other ways, often in skewed behaviors that in our culture are feminized and trivialized— eating disorders, depression, self-destructive tendencies.

Earle also saw the abuse as part of something larger, of socialized differences in power between men and women. Her counseling predecessor had gone around doing a workshop with the upbeat title of Great Sexpectations. Earle, at her workshops, showed a film called *Rethinking Rape*. And, perhaps most important, she helped start the group REACT— Rape Education Action Committee—which holds workshops critiquing the culture of rape.

"Look at the rapes in movies that are characterized as lovemaking," Earle said, giving me a sample of her teaching. "*Gone With the Wind* is a classic example. She's saying, 'No, no, no,' and he carries her upstairs, and the next morning they're in love. . . . In the socialization of boys quite often you're taught to not believe a 'no' but to push it to a 'maybe,' and then if it's a 'maybe,' maybe you can get it to a 'yes.' Or 'maybe' is 'yes.' We kind of look at that and say, 'Maybe that's not right anymore.'"

Earle's conviction that she is wrestling with a giant injustice gives her ideas a powerful, if sometimes simplistic, clarity. She is quick to condemn as "false belief" any statements that she regards as incorrect. And when she decided that an epidemic of sexual abuse on campus was being mishandled, she turned her fire on the administration that had hired her. Dartmouth's official code on sexual abuse struck her as inadequate—it "is really no definition," she said, noting that the Student Handbook contains one paragraph on sexual abuse and seven pages on alcohol. She and REACT started publicizing a truly alarming (and, as it turns out, dubious) statistic: that 125 Dartmouth women are raped every year.

From the start REACT was as dedicated to action as it was to education. The first case REACT seized upon, in the assault on the administration it launched a month after its formation in February 1990, was a curious one, given that by its own count 250 rapes had taken place on campus in the last two years. But in the end Moore Robinson's hickey made a hugely effective case.

On my second visit to Hanover, in October 1990, I heard murmured reports that an audiotape existed of REACT's March 7, 1990, rally on the steps of Parkhurst, the administration building, and, after several inquiries and a promise of secrecy, I was allowed to listen to it. The drama surrounding the tape was just a ripple of the drama of the March rally. That protest marked the day the discourse changed at Dartmouth, the moment when the winking narrative about scamming gave way to the white-lipped narrative about abuse.

REACT had organized the rally to protest the administration's "sheltering [of] rapists." The word "rape" was used over and over that afternoon. M. Moore Robinson was the star speaker. Her voice flooded with feeling as she described the contemptuous treatment she had received from the administration when, a few months before, she had filed a charge of sexual abuse.

"I'm not going to go away," she cried. "I'm going to stay here until I get rid of this scourge."

A redhead with angular features and close-cropped hair, Robinson had visited Dartmouth in spring 1988 as a prospective student—and promptly had a disturbing encounter with a burly freshman. She'd met him at a fraternity party. He'd asked her to walk with him back to his dorm. She went along, and when they got there he pulled her toward him, tried to kiss her. She struggled out of his grasp, but not before he kissed her hard on the neck.

"It's okay, you can go. I've left my mark on you," he said, according to Robinson.

Even a year and a half later, in the fall of her sophomore year at Dartmouth, the incident held great emotional resonance for Robinson. She had spoken with another woman, an alumna, who claimed to have been roughly handled by the same student. Then, in November 1989, Robinson learned that the man who'd grabbed her—Kevin Acker, now a junior—had been named editor in chief of *The Dartmouth*. With the support of Heather Earle, Robinson decided to file charges against him. (Acker told me, "I kissed her and that's it. No force was involved.")

Trying to overcome the sordid flavor of the episode . . . [the accused] portrayed it as a male fantasy of sudden sex.

Robinson openly concedes that her motives were vengeful. "I had extreme loathing for this person," she told me. "His being in a position of authority showed how completely he had gotten away with his assaults. His life was hunky-dory, while I had to live with [the attack] every day."

The administration evidently did not take the case very seriously. Dean Shanahan refused to refer the matter to the college's Committee on Standards, which can recommend suspension or expulsion, and scheduled it for a dean's hearing instead. (The punishments a dean's hearing can mete out are far lighter—requiring a student to apologize, for instance.) The disposition of the case moved Robinson to write a poem called "Rape Completed." It begins, "My welcome to dartmyth/was an attempted/rape," and ends, "Rape completed/thanks to/Parkhurst." The poem was distributed on a leaflet advertising the March 7 rally.

The picture of a woman wailing before a crowd on the administration steps about a student who grabbed her two years before suggests just how inflamed college women's sensitivities have become—and perhaps also just how powerful Heather Earle's teachings are. For years, surely, people told Moore Robinson to lighten up about the incident, and probably she tried to quash her own feelings about it. It's bracing to think of her standing in the public square at Dartmouth, across from the splendid Green, within view of the library spire and the Georgian administration buildings—all the brick and clapboard accessories of flinty New England patriarchy—holding a microphone to her mouth as she gave vent to long-bottled-up rage.

But she didn't mention Kevin Acker by name. Indeed, the speech's suspense turned on the identity of her alleged attacker. She'd be disciplined if she named him, she lamented; she was powerless to warn other women. "There's nothing I'm allowed to do," she said.

Lending a chilly drama to the occasion was the fact that Acker himself was there, standing at the edge of the crowd among a group of friends. In the *Animal House* version of events this would of course have been hugely comic. A demonstration over a hickey! What sport for the boys. But Acker was now a wanted man. And his presence turned the scene into something out of *The Scarlet Letter*.

When I [the accuser] actually spoke it had an incredibly empowering effect.

Noticing him in the crowd, Robinson seemed to lose control. On the tape her voice goes into a wail that billows out like a spinnaker of grief. She shouts, "A prime example of how completely unjust the system is is that the person who attacked me is in the audience right now! He is right here among you, and he is free to do whatever he wants, rape anyone he wants. . . ."

Acker told me he stood there stoically as people turned and searched one another's faces. But soon it was widely known on campus just who Robinson and others had meant by the "rapist." For later that day Robinson identified Acker as her alleged attacker: Emerging from the dean's office after a private meeting with Shanahan, she mentioned his name to a group of students.

Meanwhile, a few of Moore Robinson's followers decided to alert the campus population to the menace before Kevin Acker molested someone else. A group of students decided to "picket the body": At times over the next few days Acker found himself followed by three or four people holding up four fingers to indicate the number of women he was said to have in one way or another abused.

Then one morning a poster appeared on campus with Acker's picture on it: "A warning to all dartmouth womyn: beware this man." At the sides of the picture were the words "how many more ?????" and "you may be next!!!!!!"

These actions unhinged Kevin Acker. In a frenzy he called an associate dean to demand that the campus police take down the posters. She told him the First Amendment barred her from taking such a step. So he raced around campus tearing down the Xerox portrait from trees, lampposts, bulletin boards.

Shanahan blames these tactics on some REACT members. So do others on campus. When I asked Heather Earle about the poster, she grew defensive and opaque. "I certainly didn't advocate it," she said. "And that was students who did that on their own and in no way, shape, or form were connected to REACT or my position."

Changes really do happen overnight. Compared with the open air of the rest of society colleges are lab flasks.

But the REACT members to whom Earle referred me included one—Lindsay Latimore—who Kevin Acker said had followed him around campus. The next day I met Latimore for breakfast at Lou's, a campus hangout. When I asked her how Acker's name had become known around campus, she smiled broadly and turned conspiratorially toward Glenn Berry, a fellow REACT member.

Berry leaned forward to explain. "We would prefer not to talk about individual cases. It puts us in a difficult situation because it's immediately attached to REACT."

Sensational and anonymous accusation is a hallmark of the sexual-abuse movement on campuses. Brown women who had become frustrated by the administration's inaction on date-rape cases began to post a list of men's names, as many as thirty, in bathroom stalls. A man was said to have earned a place on the list after a woman identified him as having committed any of a range of acts, from date rape to harassment. In one case I know about, a student ransacked his past to locate the abuse that had gotten him billboarded and then, à la Salman Rushdie, approached the activists to find out what he had to do to have the sanction lifted.

Respect for students' civil rights does not seem to be of primary concern to the activists, not when they see human rights being abused. The literature of the campus brigades contains definitions of proper and improper speech that smack of thought control by the politically correct. "Stop fantasizing about rape," a group at the University of Wisconsin orders men in a brochure on "a rape-free culture." The Columbia-Barnard Task Force Against Sexual Coercion would restrict "offensive" remarks that "employ sexual stereotypes or generalizations" because they constitute "sexual harassment." A statement issued by the Association of American Colleges' Project on the Status and Education of Women, regarded as a leader on the issue, goes further. Under the rubric "peer harassment," it includes efforts to make women a "negative reference group"; men's domination of class discussions; and a practice called the "elephant walk," in which men expose their penis and pull out their pants pockets to portray an elephant's trunk and ears.

It may be backward to say so, but could it be that there is some charm in such an act? A self-mocking comment on one's own sexuality? When is it harassment and when is it performance art?

The key distinction for the sexual-abuse activists is whether or not an act hurts someone else's feelings. When I asked Heather Earle how to judge whether a fumbling, nonverbalized sexual encounter represented a sexual violation, she said, "I think with clumsy awkwardness . . . the woman probably isn't going to feel violated." Other activists state the corollary: If a "survivor" feels violated, then she has been violated.

This confusion of deed and emotion—and the consequent willingness to regard hurt feelings as a legitimate cause for political and disciplinary action—runs through many of the activists' arguments. It helps account for REACT's notorious assertion that 125 women are raped at Dartmouth every year—or, as REACT's statement of purpose says, "about one rape every other day!" The statistic comes from a 1989 survey of date rape at Dartmouth. Psychologist Phyllis Riggs, the former coordinator of the school's Sexual Awareness and Abuse Program, found that 8 percent of women reported having "unwanted completed sexual intercourse" during the previous year. (There are about 1,500 women at Dartmouth.) The trouble is that Riggs set out to record *feelings* of being violated: She defined "unwanted" sex to include situations in which a student, while "certain at the time that s/he did not want to engage in the sexual experience . . . did not communicate her/his unwillingness because of a feeling of intimidation."

When a community defines such an act as rape, it is formally recognizing the difference in power between men and women. It is saying, in effect, that all sexual relations take place within the context of potential violence against women. From this it follows that the individual man is always responsible for the general problem, whether or not the woman he is with expresses her fears.

The essence of this code, its underlying chemistry of power and emotion, is summed up in a recommendation from Men Stopping Rape, Inc., a group at the University of Wisconsin: The man who finds himself walking down a street behind a lone woman should go to the other side of the street in order to relieve her entirely reasonable fear that he will rape her.

Even if such an approach reflects some psychological truth, the question remains, What should a college administration, or a state, do about it? Emotion is a much weaker ground on which to define crimes than are acts or statements; deeds can't always be judged by the emotions they elicit. Feelings are not always rational or proportional. They may change over time. And there may be a genuine divide between a man's interpretation of an encounter and a woman's.

A college has to enforce rules in a way that builds consensus.

Moore Robinson's own lack of proportion may well have influenced the Dartmouth administration's disposition of her case. On March 26, 1990, nearly three weeks after the Parkhurst rally, the college broke its policy of not divulging disciplinary proceedings and published the judgment reached by an associate dean, a woman, after a two-and-a-half-hour hearing: Not guilty of abusive behavior. The administration's statements on the case mentioned no names, but just about everyone on campus knew to whom they were referring. And anyway, the next morning's issue of *The Dartmouth* seized the moment to banner Kevin Acker's innocence. Its lead story declared, "Public statement clears 'D' editor." Acker took the opportunity to sound enlightened, even statesmanlike:

"I am not unsympathetic to the issues raised concerning the way sexual assault is viewed in our society," he said. "But I deplore being used as a rallying point to advance awareness. . . . The way that [Robinson] handled this whole matter trivializes a very important topic."

Like many other women who feel that their charges of sexual abuse are not taken seriously by a college administration, Moore Robinson made plans to transfer to another school. (The following fall she went to Brown.) She told me Acker and his friends glared at her and made her uncomfortable on campus, and in one instance a red BMW carrying a group of brothers bumped into her at a crosswalk, knocking her to the ground.

She felt like a "martyr to a cause." The media had presented her case "as if he had stolen a kiss, like in the movie *Carousel*." But three weeks after the matter was dismissed, the college officially informed Acker of new charges against him, charges that were not open to such an innocent interpretation.

Charges are raised

One night in February 1990, at about the time REACT was being organized, David Lillard woke up Alma Lee with some news. He'd heard that a '92 was pressing a case against Kevin Acker before the dean's office. Recalling Lee's upset over the "scamming" two and a half years before, he thought she'd want to know.

Alma Lee was by then a junior, a member of a sorority, and a Russian studies major. Lillard's news had a dramatic effect on her. She went to Parkhurst to file a complaint of an assault. An assistant dean urged her to go to Heather Earle first. After she saw the counselor, Lee began talking to friends about the incident at great length, exploring her feelings about it, speaking of her anger, her desire to run Kevin Acker over with a car. In Earle's lexicon, Alma Lee had until now been in the "denial stage," during which a victim tries to "live her life the same way, as if the sexual assault never took place." Denial can last thirty-five years, according to Earle. The counselor helped Lee overcome what the student told me was her "self-guilt" about the incident, her feeling that she was somehow responsible for a violation of her body because she had drunk enough to lower her guard.

Days later Lee acted to "validate" her rage by speaking out at the March 7 rally on the steps of Parkhurst. Her voice is quiet and controlled on the audiotape, but there is enormous feeling behind it. "I could remain anonymous. I could let other people read my words. But when we stay silent the message to the rapist . . . is reconfirmed," she says. "The system is telling him he can do it again and again and again."

Ten days later she walked back into the dean's office with a three-page memo that began: "I am filing a complaint against Kevin Acker '91 for sexual assault." The complaint had a flowing, self-possessed tone that was to characterize all of her subsequent testimony about those moments in the Richardson men's room.

"I was aware that something was off," the statement read in part. "I thought he wanted to cut in front of me [to use the toilet]. I turned around immediately to let him know that I really had to use the toilet: thereby implying that he get out of my stall. . . . I am unclear as to whether or not I actually started to unzip my pants and sit on the toilet to urinate, because he could have already started his advances in kissing me, feeling me under my bra, putting his hands down my pants, inserting his finger, possibly two, into my vagina. . . .

"Everything seemed to be happening *to* and *at* my body so quickly, it probably lasted all of about three minutes, but my brain was processing the situation so slowly. It was not until he had his fingers in me did I realize that this person was no one that I would ever allow and consent to having his hand down there, especially since he hadn't even asked. As soon as I walked out of the stall, I felt I was walking out of a zone, waking from a nightmare. . . ."

The June 4 hearing of the Committee on Standards—closed, at Acker's request—took place in Parkhurst's South Room: a fireplace, a vast table, and a dozen people in the scrolled-arm Dartmouth armchairs. (I was able to examine a full transcript of the hearing at the Grafton County Courthouse.) The proceedings pitted an immature young man against a very mature young woman. Lee cried several times, but her story didn't substantively change. With Heather Earle at her side, serving as an advocate, Lee explained at greater length that she had been "buzzed"—by the alcohol—and slow to respond.

It is not possible to establish a bright-line distinction between aggressive behavior and sexual abuse.

Kevin Acker responded with legalisms. In a bit of swagger, he chose not to offer a written statement but to speak on his feet. He reminded the committee of the standard of proof—a preponderance of the evidence—and concluded, "It seems to me that the core issue is, Did she say anything to me—if I did make the first move, which is quite possible." He pulled out the report of the polygraph test.

Trying to overcome the sordid flavor of the episode—the ugly locale, the abrupt intimacies—Acker portrayed it as a male fantasy of sudden sex. He called it "a very unique incident in my life . . . the only time something like this has ever happened to me." She had followed him into the men's room. Wordlessly, the two began to embrace. "She took the lead, so to speak, as much as I did." She had led him into the stall. She had sat on his lap and put her hands on his shoulders. She had unzipped his pants and fondled his penis. It might have been three minutes, but it was probably eight minutes in all before someone else came into the bathroom and they agreed to stop. He had never really talked to her again.

A fifty-four-year-old classics professor on the committee named Edward J. Bradley was thoroughly perplexed. He presumed there would have to have been "already a fairly high level of erotic tension. . . . How can this explode so?"

"She didn't, you know, play with my hair or any of the traditional things you would associate with flirting," Acker said. "But our conversation throughout the entire evening was very pleasant. . . . I think that when she walked into the bathroom I did think . . . that possibly one of the reasons that she had gone in there was to do something like this, especially because it was the men's bathroom. . . . These things are seldom verbally negotiated."

Lee said Acker was lying. And if it was all so pleasant, why did her witnesses say that the incident had stunned her? ("Holding on to my coat and arm determinedly," Craig Rush testified, "she seemed somewhat nervous, almost frightened.")

The Committee of Standards found the hot-sex story implausible, and the next day, June 5, 1990, it announced a guilty verdict on the sex-abuse charge. Acker was suspended for one term. The COS would have considered a multiterm suspension had it not been for "the overall ambiguous nature of the encounter and the lack of clear communication about intentions and expectations on the part of both parties," it said in a public statement. The committee members I spoke to said that the ambiguity sprang from a few facts, on which both parties agreed, that suggested Lee had acquiesced in the early overtures. She'd put her arms on his shoulders, possibly embraced him. But, as the COS statement indicated, she'd been too drunk to express lack of consent; it cited the "presence of alcohol" in its decision to convict.

That night Alma Lee celebrated her victory at a Hanover restaurant.

Acker appealed the verdict, and on July 16, 1990, the COS held a second hearing. This time the student tried to offer an apology, but it turned into something else in his mouth: "I apologize to her now, I'm sorry that she feels bad, but . . . I didn't do anything wrong. If she thinks that I did, then this is what's going on in her mind, it's not what happened."

The committee reaffirmed its judgment, and Acker followed the tradition, established by *Dartmouth Review* students, of taking disciplinary decisions to court. When the Grafton County judge decided not to overturn Dartmouth's decision, Acker appealed to the New Hampshire Supreme Court. He was desperate to return for the the fall term, to pull off the double major and the senior thesis, to ensure the bright future in law school. But the Supreme Court refused to hear Acker's appeal.

By now, Kevin Acker had become the focal point of sexual politics on the Dartmouth campus. After the court hearing, *The Dartmouth Review* filled its front page with a photograph of Acker taken at the courthouse, a slightly blurry picture that caught him with a hint of satisfaction on his full lips. Over his head was the headline SEX OFFENDER in red ink. Five months earlier, the *Review* had observed dryly that REACT wanted nothing less from the administration than "Mr. Acker's head on a silver platter." Now it was performing that service itself.

Acker spent his term of exile in Washington, waiting tables and writing a piece on the Soviet Union for the right-wing *Policy Review*, a publication of The Heritage Foundation, which had made room for many Dartmouth students in the past. By telephone he complained to me that the sex-abuse standard at Dartmouth overlooked the fact that women play an active role in sex. "It is clear that the entire burden to determine whether Ms. Lee was a willing participant in the encounter fell on me."

If a case such as this one could be said to have a winner, it would have to be Alma Lee. She had been on leave when I visited Dartmouth; I spoke to her by telephone after she got back to Hanover in January. She agreed to speak only after I explained that I did not intend to identify her. She told me that the rally on the steps of Parkhurst had marked a turning point for her. "When I actually spoke it had an incredibly empowering effect." Afterward, the campus had given her enormous support.

The woman on the phone seemed only more mature and focused than the woman of the tape and transcripts. Alma Lee was planning on going to law school, she was going to do what she could on women's issues. She said, "I'd like to direct all the emotions I feel about these things into something that will work in our system, instead of being angry."

A changed world

The campus Kevin Acker came back to in January 1991 was, on its surface anyway, thoroughly changed. An administration task force was calling for more funds for the Sexual Awareness and Abuse Program. REACT members now spoke of the Dartmouth administration as "progressive." It was easy to see why campuses have historically been so attractive to reformers. Changes really do happen overnight. Compared with the open air of the rest of society colleges are lab flasks. A few energetic people who know what they believe can turn everything around in a semester.

No doubt Dartmouth is now a more hospitable place for women. Petty assaults are more likely to be rebuked. There will be fewer "atrocities." It's possible that campuses like this one will lead the rest of society to a recognition of the seriousness of date rape.

Of course, one way to accomplish that would be by prosecuting cases such as Acker's in criminal courts rather than before campus committees. The question remains why this was not done in this instance. Alma Lee herself cited New Hampshire's sexual-assault statute during the COS hearings, and Dartmouth later argued in court that Acker's "conduct would constitute aggravated felonious sexual assault."

Quite possibly Alma Lee could have persuaded a jury of that. But both students and administrators at Dartmouth recoiled at the idea of prosecution, in part because victims have a hard enough time confiding in deans, let alone D.A.'s. "They might say, 'I don't want to go in front of an open courtroom; I'd rather just do it in front of five or seven college people,'" Heather Earle told me. (Of course, no such option is available to the nineteen-year-old who doesn't go to college.) Dean Shanahan explained that a college has to enforce rules in a way that builds consensus, "in a way that is organically connected to the nature of the institution. It has to preserve the very fragile community. It's not like a society where somebody can move from one state to the next. You have to come back into the same classroom, into the same dormitory."

The dean's picture might be more convincing if Kevin Acker had been afforded any such sensitivity. But, of course, his face went up on trees. And the administration not only issued two statements to students on the matter (no names, it's true, but everyone knew to whom they referred) but also mailed the court decisions in the case to reporters. Acker was made a symbol and a cause, forced to endure the opprobrium and publicity of a criminal defendant but without the benefit of the greater thoroughness of a trial. (He could not, for instance, cross-examine witnesses.) There did not seem to be much empathy for Acker as a member of the "fragile community." When I suggested to Heather Earle that a student found guilty of abuse should perhaps be forced to work in a rape clinic, be encouraged to learn from his error, she demurred strongly. She offered the example of "men who assault children," who get their therapy in prison.

If REACT had used the Acker case to promote its agenda, so had the Dartmouth administration. By publicizing its actions, it sought to publicize its new, enlightened image to the world and to clarify norms of sexual interaction among its students. "A consensus . . . is only now emerging about what the elements of abuse are," Shanahan told me. The new rule was, You couldn't go ahead with sex without a "yes." I remembered what Acker had said in court and had to agree. The requirement of a "yes" seemed to skate over the true dynamics of an encounter, the unspoken give-and-take. Over the telephone, Shanahan interpreted the rule for me: "A misreading of my 'No means no' would be to put quotation marks around those words. When we say, 'No means no' and 'The absence of a yes means no,' that doesn't mean the absence of a verbalized yes means no. There is the courting, there is the initiation of an activity, and the response. It's the nature of the response that indicates the yes or the no. For example, if I am engaging in suggestive intimacies with somebody and touch that person, I don't need to get a yes, I don't need to ask permission. That occurs within the context of what's happened just prior to it. What is the response that I get to that? Does that suggest that it is accepted or not?"

The dean's difficulty in spelling out this standard suggests that it is not possible to establish a bright-line distinction between aggressive behavior and sexual abuse; it is a matter of degree.

My conversations with college men and women indicate that, despite the change in the official climate, late-night behavior has not really changed that much. "For society to hold men or women to that standard [an explicit 'yes'] is absurd," said Jim Morris, who served as a senior on the COS that convicted Acker. "There's a social dance that goes on. Passivity you read as acceptance rather than denial." It's easy for Morris to say that now: He graduated and lives on the West Coast. Back in Hanover, the new orthodoxy does not encourage such thinking or, at least, speaking.

Indeed, the conversation about sexual mores at Dartmouth had become too brittle, and perhaps too fearful, to admit such arguments. "There'd have been an explosion if he had been let off," Morris told me, recalling the atmosphere on campus. The speed and fury with which so many different factions battened on Kevin Acker suggest that he had presented a convenient and irresistible villain. Rather than explore the ambiguities of the issue, it had been much easier for everybody concerned to demonize Kevin Acker, to say, *We're nothing like him.* Kevin Acker, who served so ably in the role of everybody's Other, had brought a certain clarity to a clouded realm.

7

A Radical Feminist View of Rape

Lois Copeland and Leslie R. Wolfe

Lois Copeland is publications director and Leslie R. Wolfe is president of the Center for Women Policy Studies.

The question of rape is synergistically related to the more fundamental issue of society's being patriarchal, with misogyny its supporting cornerstone. Violence (especially rape) and the threat of violence against women are useful instruments for maintaining male dominance. It follows that unless laws, male behavioral patterns, and societal perceptions are radically altered to create a genuine gender equity, being female with always remain a risk factor.

- You're a bunch of fucking feminists!" the gunman shouted. He then ordered the women to line up against one wall and opened fire with a 22-caliber automatic rifle. Fourteen women were killed (Russell and Caputi, 1990).
- He hammered his girlfriend's left temple once with a claw hammer, he then swung the hammer in an arc twice more; this time "her head split open like a watermelon." Thirty-five days later he was out on bail, taking college courses (Harrison, 1982).
- "I remember countless episodes of how my husband blackened my eyes, bloodied my lips, how he dislocated my shoulder . . . how I miscarried our child after he beat me. I left three times, each time he threatened to injure or kill members of my family to get me to return home. I stayed with him out of fear" (Baer, 1990).
- She has a few drinks and flirts with some patrons at a bar. Suddenly she finds herself held down while six young men rape her as onlookers cheer them on. Their defense was that she acted seductively and "led them on" (Karmen, 1990).
- Rachel attends a party in her dorm at a big university. A football player, an acquaintance, asks her to come to his room down the hall. He assaults her, not listening to her protests to stop. The next day he comes to her room and asks her out. He felt the behavior the preceding evening was normal (Warshaw, 1988).
- The female student is invited to a frat party. Alcohol is plentiful.

She is encouraged to drink and is taken to a room where a "train"[1] of men have sex with her (Sanday, 1990).

Sexism and violence against women: Crimes of misogyny

These cases are snapshots of the kind of violence against women that occurs daily throughout the United States and the world. To understand the nature and extent of this violence, we first must look at the culture of domination and patriarchy against which women's movements worldwide have struggled for many years; indeed, "the U. S. social change movement on behalf of abused women is entering its third decade" (Chapman, 1990). Throughout these past two decades, feminist theorists have written extensively about violence against women,[2] which is seen as the quintessential example of sex discrimination and sexual oppression —as the most powerful tool of male domination and patriarchal control.[3] As Charlotte Bunch has recently reiterated:

> Sex discrimination kills women daily. When combined with race, class, and other forms of oppression, it constitutes a deadly denial of women's right to life and liberty on a large scale throughout the world. The most pervasive violation of females is violence against women in all its manifestations, from wife battery, incest, and rape, to dowry deaths, genital mutilation, and female sexual slavery (Bunch, 1990).

Violence—and the internalized and constant threat of violence—is seen as an instrument of control, keeping women "in their place." As with other hate crimes, violence against each woman terrorizes and intimidates the entire class—all women.

The threat of violence permeates every aspect of women's lives. It alters where women live, work, and study, as they try to be safe by staying within certain prescribed bounds.

Women learn these rules when they are girls; they learn to "protect" themselves by restricting their lives, to "be careful" and to accept the blame when their precautions fail. In short, women learn their "place" and their fear very early.

Women—whether they are white or women of color, heterosexual or lesbian, young or old—know that they cannot go to places men can go without the fear of being attacked and violated. Campuses, parking lots, libraries, shopping centers, parks, jogging trails—all are possible danger zones. And, even when women stay within society's prescribed bounds their safety is not assured; studies have shown that women often are most at risk with their intimate partners or friends (Browne, 1987).

Women also learn (as do men) the cultural myths about violence against women which continue to victimize women and which, in large part, still shape our attitudes. These myths suggest that woman battering and rape are "crimes of passion," that wife abuse is a "private, family affair," and that women who are battered, raped, or killed "had it coming" because of some fault or error of their own. Even when violence against women is defined as a societal rather than a personal problem, it does not receive the level of serious attention that other violations of individual freedom or of civil and human rights receive.[4]

Such attitudes are woven throughout the fabric of our society, and violence against women still is portrayed as acceptable and inevitable in many subtle and overt ways. These attitudes are so deeply ingrained that a Rhode Island Rape Crisis Center survey of 1,700 sixth- to ninth-grade students in 1988 found that a substantial percentage of these pre-adolescents and adolescents believed that a man has the right to kiss or have sexual intercourse with a woman against her will, particularly if he has "spent money on her." Half of the students said that a woman who walks alone at night and dresses "seductively" is "asking to be raped" (Mann, 1988).

As men absorb and accept their patriarchal rights of ownership of women and children, they also may assume their right to control and demand obedience from their partners (and often their unmarried female relatives as well) and even to use force to ensure it. Indeed, the English Common Law's "rule of thumb"[5] is evidence of longstanding legal and political support for such violence (Holtzman, 1986). Cultural support reaffirms it, as "men who assault their wives are actually living up to cultural prescriptions that are cherished in Western society—aggressiveness, male dominance, and female subordination—and they are using physical force as a means to enforcing that dominance" (Dobash and Dobash, 1979).

Battered women who seek to break the cycle and free themselves from abusive relationships still confront sexist assumptions that further victimize them. In court, battered women often are blamed for the abuse and its seriousness is minimized—suggesting that such violence is a normal expression of male dominance. Examples are legion, as the women who operate shelters for battered women and the attorneys who represent them can attest; in one case, for instance, the judge hearing her divorce case told a battered woman—who had suffered physical and mental abuse during 23 years of marriage—"that he thought she was lying and that he could not believe that her husband, an upstanding citizen, would beat her unless she 'had it coming'" (Supreme Court [MI], 1989).

Women who are raped are further victimized by cultural myths infused into the legal system (Smart, 1989) and by rape laws that were based on patriarchal assumptions about female sexuality and men's rights. Women who are raped must defend themselves from the suggestion that they consented to violent sexual intercourse by "contributory behavior"—by saying "no" but meaning "yes," by wearing "seductive" clothes, by having had a prior sexual history, by going to "dangerous" places (a bar, a campus fraternity party, Central Park). In short, women must confront the assumption that most men do not rape and that most women bring it on themselves.

Acquaintance rape, like wife abuse, is still defined as a woman's personal problem. The myth that rape is a crime of sexually aroused and violent strangers—not "normal" men, not friends or dates or partners—further punishes women. It is assumed that the existence of any prior relationship (even if it is a recent acquaintanceship) suggests consent and that a man is entitled to sexual control of a woman. Acquaintance and date rapes thus are trivialized and hidden. Indeed, young women who report such assaults on campuses often find themselves doubly punished for raising the issue.[6]

While stranger rape and acquaintance rape are both considered rape, the differences in attitude and prosecution are monumental. Men who know their victims are least likely to be arrested, prosecuted, and convicted. Where there is so-called "contributory behavior" by the woman, juries are less likely to convict. An aggravated rape—defined as one in which there are multiple assailants, the rape is accompanied by additional violence, or the rapist uses a weapon—will more likely result in a conviction. Indeed, while theoretically all rapes are investigated and prosecuted to the fullest extent of the law, in reality if a woman is raped by a stranger—especially if a weapon has been used and/or the alleged rapist is a man of color while the victim is white, thus reflecting the extent of race and sex bias combined—she is more likely to be believed and to see him prosecuted and convicted (Estrich, 1987).

Finally, while male murder victims are likely to be murdered as a result of felonious activities or during alcohol- or drug-influenced brawls (Federal Bureau of Investigation, 1990), women are most likely to be murdered simply because they are women. Many murders of women are classic examples of gender-biased hate crimes; the term "femicide," used most recently by Jane Caputi and Diana Russell (1990), refers to the political murders of women who are killed solely because they are women and reflects a theoretical analysis of these crimes as gender-biased hate crimes. Perhaps the most obvious case of such a political crime is the Montreal murders committed by Marc Lepine; before he murdered fourteen women engineering students, he expressed his hatred of them as "feminists" who had gained entry into the male-dominated field that he could not. Their visibility in this field increased his anger and hatred of all women; not only did he resent their success, he also blamed their presence for his failure to be admitted to the engineering program. It is a classic case.

But it is not the only one. Although murder, the ultimate crime of violence, affects both women and men, many murders of women can be seen as the final expression of patriarchal values of sexual domination (Caputi, 1987). For example, all recorded serial murderers have been men and the large majority kill women (Caputi, 1987); in addition, they frequently bind, rape, and torture their victims before they murder them.

Feminist analysts and activists against violence all insist that violence against women must no longer be defined solely as a crime against an individual who happens to be female and is unfortunate enough to become a victim. Rather, this violence must be seen for what it is—a crime of misogyny, of hatred of women. While not every man beats his female partner or rapes women, feminist theorists would suggest that society's acceptance of patriarchal assumptions and structures also accepts and condones these violations of women's autonomy. The evidence is in the fact that women worldwide "are routinely subject to torture, starvation, terrorism, humiliation, mutilation, and even murder simply because they are female" (Bunch, 1990).

"The message," Charlotte Bunch reminds us, "is domination; stay in your place or be afraid. Contrary to the argument that such violence is only personal or cultural, it is profoundly political. It results from the structural relationships of power, domination, and privilege between men and women in society. Violence against women is central to maintaining those political relations at home, at work, and in all public spheres" (Bunch, 1990).

This viewpoint takes the next step in this analysis—placing violence against women in the context of widely accepted definitions of bias-motivated hate crimes. We seek to show that acts of violence based on gender—like acts of violence based on race, ethnicity, national origin, religion, and sexual identity—are not random, isolated acts. Rather, these are crimes against individuals that are meant to intimidate and terrorize the larger group or class of people—women.

Women are not safe on the streets

- In 1984, 2.3 million violent crimes (rape, assault, and robbery) were committed against women over the age of 12 (Select Committee on Children, Youth, and Families, 1987).
- In 1988 the FBI received reports of 92,486 forcible rapes of women over the age of 12; only 20 percent to 40 percent were stranger rapes (FBI, 1987).
- In 1982, 4,118 serial murders were reported; the majority of the victims were women (Caputi, 1987).

- Two hundred three rape cases, many involving prostitutes or women who used drugs, were dropped by the Oakland (CA) Police Department without even minimal investigation (Gross, 1990).
- Since 1974, the rate of reported assaults against women ages 20 to 24 has risen by 48 percent, but assault rates against young men in the same age group declined by 12 percent (Committee on the Judiciary, 1990).

Women are not safe in their homes

- Every 15 seconds a woman is beaten by her husband or boyfriend (Bureau of Justice Statistics, 1986).
- Thirty percent of women who are homicide victims are killed by their husbands or boyfriends (FBI, 1986).
- Each year, 4,000 women are killed in the context of domestic violence situations—by husbands or partners who have abused them (Stark, 1981).

- One in four—25 percent—of women who attempted suicide had been victims of family violence (Browne, 1987).
- One in seven women in a San Francisco sample reportedly were raped by their husbands (Russell, 1990).
- Nearly nine percent of college women who are raped are raped by family members (Select Committee on Children, Youth, and Families, 1990).

Women are not always safe with their friends

- Rape crisis centers report that 70 to 80 percent of all rapes are committed by acquaintances of the women (Warshaw, 1985).
- A study of 2,291 adult working women found that 39 percent of rapes were committed by husbands, part-

ners, or relatives; only 17 percent were committed by total strangers (Koss, 1990).
- According to a national study, 84 percent of women who had been raped knew their attackers (Ageton, 1983).

Women are not safe on college campuses

- In a survey of 3,187 college women, 478 reported having been raped; of these, 10.6 percent were raped by strangers, 24.9 percent were raped by non-romantic acquaintances, 21 percent were raped by casual dates, and 30 percent were raped by steady dates (Koss, Gidycz, and Wisniewski, 1987).
- One out of every four college women is attacked by a rapist before she graduates; one in seven will be raped (Koss, 1990).
- More than half of college rape victims are attacked by dates (Koss, 1990), and studies of high school and college students conducted during the 1980s reported rates of dating violence ranging from 12 to 65 percent (Levy, 1990).
- The number of college women raped in 1986 was 14 times higher than officially reported in the National Crime Survey (Koss, 1990).

Women are not safe from sexual harassment at school, at work, and on the streets

- A government survey revealed that 42 percent of female respondents working in federal government agencies reported that they had been harassed during a two-year period from 1985 to 1987 (Chapman, 1988).
- A survey of women psychology graduates found that 17 percent had sexual contact with a professor while they were working towards their degree (Project on the Status and Education of Women, 1986).
- Virtually every woman has been subject to some form of street harassment, in which individual men or groups of men whistle, make sexual comments or slurs, issue sexual invitations, or yell obscenities at women passing by (Hughes and Sandler, 1988).

Data collection and the meaning of statistics

The very pervasiveness of violence against women—reflected in available statistics, inadequate as they may be—documents the extent to which "the risk factor is being female" (Heise, 1989). Department of Justice figures show overwhelmingly that reported crimes against women are increasing while crimes against men are decreasing. According to a recent study published by the Committee on the Judiciary of the US Senate, the rate of sexual assaults is now increasing four times faster than the overall crime rate, and the number of reported rapes reached 100,000 in the United States in 1990 (Majority Staff, Committee on the Judiciary, 1991). Since 1974, assaults against young women have risen by an astounding 50 percent, while assaults against young men have dropped by 12 percent (Congressional Caucus on Women's Issues, 1990). Many women live in fear of violence not only on the streets but in their own homes.

Statistics do more than demonstrate how widespread violence against women truly is in our society. They tell us that women are not safe anywhere, from anyone. In the larger sense, as Susan Schechter has stated, "violence against women robs women of possibilities, self-confidence, and self-esteem. In this sense, violence is more than a physical assault; it is an attack on women's dignity and freedom" (Schechter, 1982). And each act of violence against a single woman intimidates and terrifies all women.

These are not isolated random instances of violence in our homes and on the streets. Yet as compelling as the statistics on reported crimes are, they represent a substantial undercount of actual violence against women, for a variety of reasons. Many women's anti-violence groups believe that violence against women is minimized because women's lives are not valued and the violence is so commonplace (Pharr, 1990). Perhaps for similar reasons, women often do not report incidents of rape and battering.

National studies indicate that as many as four million women are battered each year, but only about 48 percent of cases are reported to police (Langan and Innes, 1986). Battered women do not report abuse for many reasons. Women face the legitimate fear that their partners will carry out their threats of retaliatory violence or loss of access to their children if they report the crime or leave the relationship. Indeed, much evidence suggests that a woman is in the greatest danger when she tries to leave her abuser (Browne, 1987). In addition, as substantial research has reported during the past two decades, many battered women are economically dependent on their abusive partners and many still suffer from the constellation of beliefs and feelings now defined as "battered woman syndrome" (King, 1984). And finally, a woman may believe (with justification) that the criminal justice system will trivialize her reports of abuse and be unable or unwilling to protect her (National Center for State Courts, 1990).

Furthermore, only 7 percent of all rapes are reported to police and fewer than 5 percent of college women report incidents of rape to the police; more than half of raped college women tell *no one* of their assaults. According to Koss, Woodruff, and Koss (1990), FBI studies corroborate these findings, reporting that 10 percent of rapes and sexual assaults are reported to police; by comparison, the reporting rate for robbery is 53 percent, for assault it is 46 percent, and for burglary it is 52 percent.

Federal data collection: Flaws in the system

But even if all women who had been raped or battered were to report the crimes to police, accurate data still would be unavailable, because of the manner in which the federal government compiles crime statistics. The US Department of Justice administers two statistical programs to measure crime in the United States: the Uniform Crime Reporting (UCR) Program and the National Crime Survey (NCS). Because of differences in methodology and crime coverage, the results from these two data collection programs are not strictly comparable or consistent (Klaus and Rand, 1984).

The Federal Bureau of Investigation (FBI) administers the UCR Program, which collects information on crimes reported to law enforcement authorities in the following categories: homicide, forcible rape, robbery, aggravated assault, burglary, larceny-theft, motor vehicle theft, and arson.

These reports, however, do not include a category for reporting cases of domestic violence, thus suggesting that it is not a "crime" in the eyes of the FBI. In addition, offense data on crimes that may be family violence, such as non-aggravated assault, are not reported to the FBI. Also, data about relationships between the victim and the offender, including familial relationships, are collected only for the crime of homicide.[7] Thus, it is impossible to use national statistics from police departments to determine the extent of family violence, including rape.

The Bureau of Justice Statistics' National Crime Survey (NCS) collects detailed information on the frequency and nature of crimes, whether or not those crimes are reported to law enforcement agencies. The NCS survey is based on an extensive, scientifically selected sample of approximately 100,000 American households (Bureau of Justice Statistics, 1989). Theoretically, the survey could provide statistical information on various aspects of violence against women. But, because the survey is not specifically designed to address the sensitive nature of sexual assault and woman abuse, this is virtually impossible; for example, the NCS does not code "spouse" and "ex-spouse" separately (Klaus and Rand, 1984), thus making it impossible to determine how many divorced or separated women continue to be abused once they leave the marriage.

Women who are raped are further victimized . . . by rape laws that were based on patriarchal assumptions about female sexuality and men's rights.

In addition, problems with the methodology of the NCS data collection system affect the accuracy of all data, but particularly data on rape (Koss, 1990). Koss suggests that those problems originate with the interview methodology: interviews are not conducted in private; the interviewers are not matched by gender or race/ethnicity to interviewees; the rape screening question and the follow-up questions are inadequate; the UCR definition of rape that serves as the foundation of the NCS definition is too narrow and is inconsistent with state statutes and federal rape law; and multiple incidents of rape involving the same persons are excluded from the calculation of victimization rates in the NCS. This distorts the picture of rape because acquaintance rape is more likely than stranger rape to involve multiple incidents; thus, the NCS survey exaggerates the incidence of stranger rape and interracial rape (Koss, 1990), as compared to acquaintance and familial rape.

According to Steven R. Schlesinger, Director of the Bureau of Justice Statistics, "neither of these two methods is particularly well-suited to estimating the incidence of family violence, so the figures presented here (about 450,000) cannot and, in fact, should not be used to estimate directly the extent of family violence in the United States." On the subject of rape, he suggested that "it is indeed unfortunate that even with the benefits of the elegant and expensive survey technology employed in the NCS an accurate picture of rape fails to emerge from the NCS. Rather than being revealed, the true incidence of rape is covered up by these data" (Koss, 1990).

Although the NCS does not plan any changes in methodology or definitions,[8] the Justice Department has begun to address some data collection problems in the FBI's Uniform Crime Reporting (UCR) Program, by implementing the National Incident-Based Reporting System (NIBRS). This system should increase the degree of detail in the reporting of criminal offenses. According to the Justice Department, more will be known about when and where crime takes place, what form it takes, and the characteristics of its victims and perpetrators (Federal Bureau of Investigation, 1988). Data are expected to be more accurate and detailed. For example, domestic violence will be added to the list of reportable offenses; further, the age, sex, race, ethnicity and relationship of the victim will be correlated with those of the offender.

Along with improving data collection methods, the UCR is revising several definitions listed in the Crime Index. Rape, for example, was defined narrowly as "the carnal knowledge of a female forcibly and against her will." The definition has been broadened in NIBRS to include "the carnal knowledge of a person, forcibly and/or against that person's will; or, not forcibly or against the person's will where the victim is incapable of giving consent because of his/her temporary or permanent mental or physical incapacity." Although not ideal, the expanded definition allows a larger number of sexual assaults, including same sex rapes, to be recorded as such.

Each act of violence against a single woman intimidates and terrifies all women.

In addition, new definitions have been devised for rape offenses which had not been previously reported, such as "forcible sodomy," "sexual assault with an object," and "forcible fondling." The revised definitions of rape and the new definitions incorporated in NIBRS may improve data collection in sexual assault and domestic violence cases. However, this improvement will come slowly, when each state is ready to comply; while a few states already are prepared and are waiting for the program to be put in place, others may not be ready for eight to ten years. Unfortunately, until all states have changed over to NIBRS the UCR (FBI) will continue to publish its annual report, *Crimes in the United States*, with incomplete data; a second report of NIBRS data also will be published.

In short, despite some optimism about these proposed changes, we still must rely upon official statistics on crimes against women published by the FBI and the Bureau of Justice Statistics that underestimate, do not accurately report, or do not report at all on the extent of violence against women. While revisions have been made to update the reporting of crimes in general and crimes against women in particular, much more needs to be done to portray the scope of anti-woman violence.

Endnotes

1. "Pulling train" or "gang banging" refers to a group of men lining up like train cars to take turns having sex with the same woman. "Bernice Sandler recently reported that she had found more than seventy-five documented cases of gang rape (pulling train or gang banging) on college campuses in recent years" (Sanday, 1990, p. 1).

2. See Eva Figes (1970), who suggests that the "motivation for male domination is the idea of paternity . . . [as man] saw himself as the physical father of the child [woman] bears . . . himself as creator, woman [as] mere vessel. Since no man can control all men, it is primarily the woman he must control, mentally/physically" (p. 34).

Susan Brownmiller (1975) links rape and patriarchy; also see Andrea Dworkin (1974), Catharine MacKinnon (1989), and Kate Millett (1970), for example. bell hooks (1990) writes that "both groups [white men and Black men] have been socialized to condone patriarchal affirmation of rape as an acceptable way to maintain male domination. It is the merging of sexuality with male domination within patriarchy that informs the construction of masculinity for men of all races and classes" (p. 59).

3. "Patriarchy is the ideology and sexism the system that holds it in place" (Pharr, 1988, p. 8).

4. See Charlotte Bunch's excellent analysis: "Despite a clear record of deaths and demonstrable abuse, women's rights are not commonly classified as human rights. This is problematic both theoretically and practically, because it has grave consequences for the way society views and treats the fundamental issues of women's lives" (Bunch, 1990, p. 486).

5. "In addition to sexual domination and control, men were granted ownership rights to physically abuse their wives. The expression 'rule of thumb' comes from the tradition embodied in common law that made it legal for a man to beat his wife as long as the stick used was not bigger around than his thumb" (Holtzman, 1986, p. 1435).

6. Testifying before the Senate Judiciary Committee, a young woman described being raped on her college campus and being further victimized by the institution's response. While a first-year student at a small college, she was raped by a male friend who had offered to walk her home after a fraternity party. For a week following the assault she talked to no one, skipping classes and meals; later, with the help of a friend, she sought help from a school counselor, who told her to "keep her grades up" so she could transfer colleges and not to press charges. As a result, the rapist's name was never revealed and he went on to rape several other "friends" while in college (testimony before Senate Judiciary Committee, August 29, 1990).

7. According to a spokesperson from the National Victims Resource Center, "a Bureau of Justice Statistics statistician has been asking for years to compile accurate statistics on domestic violence victims."

8. The wording of some of the screening questions pertaining to rape was changed several years ago; NCS is waiting for the results of these changes to show up on 1990 data before making further changes.

References

Ageton, S. S. (1983). *Sexual assault among adolescents: A national study*. Final report submitted to the National Institute of Mental Health.

Baer, S. (1990, October 2). Freedom from fear. *Baltimore Sun*, C-1.

Browne, A. (1987). *When battered women kill*. New York: The Free Press.

Brownmiller, S. (1975). *Against our will: Men, women, and rape*. New York: Simon and Schuster.

Bunch, C. (1990). Women's rights as human rights: Toward a re-vision of human rights. *Human Rights Quarterly, 12*, 486-98.

Bureau of Justice Statistics. (1989). *Criminal victimization in the United States*. Washington, DC: US Department of Justice.

Caputi, J. (1987). *The age of sex crime*. Bowling Green, OH: Bowling Green State University Popular Press.

Caputi, J. and Russell, D. E. H. (1990, September/October). "Femicide": Speaking the unspeakable. *Ms.*, 35.

Chapman, G. (1988). Sexual harassment of women in federal employment. *Response, 11*, (2), 26.

Chapman, J. R. (1990, Summer). Violence against women as a violation of human rights. *Social Justice, 17*, (2), 54-70.

Committee on the Judiciary, US Senate. (1990, October 2). *Violence Against Women Act Of 1990*, Report 101-545. Washington, DC: Committee on the Judiciary.

Congressional Caucus on Women's Issues. (1990, July). *Violence against women*. Washington, DC: CCWI.

Dobash, R. E. and Dobash, R. (1979). *Violence against wives*. New York: The Free Press.

Dworkin, A. (1974). *Woman hating*. New York: Dutton.

Estrich, S. (1987). *Real rape*. Cambridge, MA: Harvard University Press.

Federal Bureau of Investigation. (1990, 1987). *Uniform crime reports for the United States*. Washington, DC: US Department of Justice.

Federal Bureau of Investigation. (1988, July). Uniform crime reporting: National incident-based reporting system, Vol 1, Data Collection Guidelines. Washington, DC: US Department of Justice.

Federal Bureau of Investigation. (1986). *Crime in the United States*. Washington, DC: US Department of Justice.

Figes, E. (1970). *Patriarchal attitudes*. Greenwich, CT: Fawcett.

Gross, J. (1990, September 20). 203 rape cases reopened in Oakland as the police chief admits mistakes. *The New York Times*, 14.

Harrison, B. G. (1982, September). The Yale murder: Poor Richard and "the girl he couldn't share." *Ms.*, 85.

Heise, L. (1989). International dimensions of violence against women. *Response, 12*, (1), 3-11.

Holtzman, E. (1986, October). Women and the law. *Villanova Law Review, 31*, 1429-1438.

hooks, b. (1990). *Yearning*. Boston: South End Press.

Hughes, J. O. and Sandler, B. R. (1988). *Peer harassment: Hassles for women on campus*. Washington, DC: Association of American Colleges.

Karmen, A. (1990). *Crime victims*. Pacific Grove, CA: Brooks/Cole.

King, N. R. (1984, Fall). Book review: The battered woman syndrome. *Response, 7*, (4), 28.

Klaus, P. A. and Rand, M. R. (1984, April). *Family violence*. Washington, DC: Bureau of Justice Statistics.

Koss, M. P. (1990, August 29). Rape incidence: A review and assessment of the data. Testimony presented to the Committee on the Judiciary, US Senate.

Koss, M. P., Gidycz, C. A, and Wisniewski, N. (1987). The scope of rape: Incidence and prevalence of sexual aggression and victimization in a national sample of higher education students. *Journal of Consulting and Clinical Psychology, 55*, 162-170.

Koss, M. P., Woodruff, W. V., and Koss, P. (1990, August). *A criminological study: Statistics on sexual violence against women.* Unpublished manuscript.

Langan, P. and Innes, C. (1986, August). *Preventing domestic violence against women, special report.* Washington, DC: Bureau of Justice Statistics, US Department of Justice.

Levy, B. (1990). Abusive teen dating relationships. *Response, 13,* (1), 5.

MacKinnon, C. (1989). *Toward a feminist theory of the state.* Cambridge, MA: Harvard University Press.

Majority Staff, Committee on the Judiciary, United States Senate. (1991, March 21). *Violence against women: The increase of rape in America 1990.* Washington, DC: Committee on the Judiciary.

Mann, J. (1988, May 6). Twisted attitudes taint youth. *Washington Post,* D3.

Millett, K. (1970). *Sexual politics.* Garden City, NY: Doubleday.

National Center for State Courts. (1990). *Proceedings of the national conference on gender bias in the courts.* Williamsburg, VA: NCSC.

Pharr, S. (1988). *Homophobia: A weapon of sexism.* Inverness, CA: Chardon Press.

Pharr, S. (1990, January). Hate violence against women. *Transformation, 5,* (1), 1.

Project on the Status and Education of Women, Association of American Colleges. (1986, Summer). Sex with professor not a good idea in retrospect. *On Campus With Women, 16,* (1), 3.

Russell, D. E. H. (1990). *Rape in marriage.* Bloomington: Indiana University Press.

Russell, D. E. H. and Caputi, J. (1990, March-April). Canadian massacre. *New Directions for Women, 19,* (2),17.

Sanday, P. (1990). *Fraternity gang rape.* New York: New York University Press.

Schechter, S. (1982). *Women and male violence.* Boston: South End Press.

Select Committee on Children, Youth, and Families. (1987, September 16). *Hearing on women, violence, and the law.* Washington, DC: US House of Representatives.

Smart, C. (1989). *Feminism and the power of law.* London and New York: Routledge.

Stark, E. and others. (1981). Wife abuse in the medical setting: An introduction for health personnel. *National Clearinghouse on Domestic Violence, Monograph Series No. 7.* Washington, DC: US Government Printing Office.

Supreme Court of Michigan. (1989, December). *Final report of the Michigan Supreme Court task force on gender issues in the courts.* Lansing, MI: Supreme Court.

Warshaw, R. (1988). *I never called it rape.* New York: Harper and Row.

8

A Critique of "Rape-Crisis" Feminists

Katie Roiphe

Katie Roiphe was a doctoral candidate in English literature at Princeton University when this article was adapted from her book The Morning After: Sex, Fear and Feminism on Campus.

"Rape-crisis" feminists are betraying many of the principles of feminism. In fact, many campus rape activists, by eliminating the distinction between rape and a bad sexual experience, are unwittingly perpetuating stereotypes of women as weak, innocent, and easily preyed upon by stronger, lascivious men. The perpetuation of myths of this kind, namely that women are the weaker, innocent sex, only succeeds in keeping women in the nineteenth-century prisons from which feminism should be liberating them.

One in four college women has been the victim of rape or attempted rape. One in four. I remember standing outside the dining hall in college, looking at a purple poster with this statistic written in bold letters. It didn't seem right. If sexual assault was really so pervasive, it seemed strange that the intricate gossip networks hadn't picked up more than one or two shadowy instances of rape. If I was really standing in the middle of an "epidemic," a "crisis"—if 25 percent of my women friends were really being raped—wouldn't I know it? These posters were not presenting facts. They were advertising a mood. Preoccupied with issues like date rape and sexual harassment, campus feminists produce endless images of women as victims—women offended by a professor's dirty joke, women pressured into sex by peers, women trying to say no but not managing to get it across.

This portrait of the delicate female bears a striking resemblance to that 50's ideal my mother and other women of her generation fought so hard to leave behind. They didn't like her passivity, her wide-eyed innocence. They didn't like the fact that she was perpetually offended by sexual innuendo. They didn't like her excessive need for protection. She represented personal, social and intellectual possibilities collapsed, and they worked and marched, shouted and wrote to make her irrelevant for their daughters. But here she is again, with her pure intentions and her wide eyes. Only this time it is the feminists themselves who are breathing new life into her.

Is there a rape crisis on campus? Measuring rape is not as straightforward as it might seem. Neil Gilbert, a professor of social welfare at the University of California at Berkeley, questions the validity of the one-in-four statistic. Gilbert points out that in a 1985 survey undertaken by *Ms.* magazine and financed by the National Institute of Mental Health, 73 percent of the women categorized as rape victims did not initially define their experience as rape; it was Mary Koss, the psychologist conducting the study, who did.

One of the questions used to define rape was: "Have you had sexual intercourse when you didn't want to because a man gave you alcohol or drugs?" The phrasing raises the issue of agency. Why aren't college women responsible for their own intake of alcohol or drugs? A man may give her drugs, but she herself decides to take them. If we assume that women are not all helpless and naïve, then they should be held responsible for their choice to drink or take drugs. If a woman's "judgment is impaired" and she has sex, it isn't necessarily always the man's fault; it isn't necessarily always rape.

As Gilbert delves further into the numbers, he does not necessarily disprove the one-in-four statistic, but he does clarify what it means—the so-called rape epidemic on campuses is more a way of interpreting, a way of seeing, than a physical phenomenon. It is more about a change in sexual politics than a change in sexual behavior. Whether or not one in four college women has been raped, then, is a matter of opinion, not a matter of mathematical fact.

If 25 percent of my women friends were really being raped—wouldn't I know it?

That rape is a fact in some women's lives is not in question. It's hard to watch the solemn faces of young Bosnian girls, their words haltingly translated, as they tell of brutal rapes; or to read accounts of a suburban teen-ager raped and beaten while walking home from a shopping mall. We all agree that rape is a terrible thing, but we no longer agree on what rape is. Today's definition has stretched beyond bruises and knives, threats of death or violence to include emotional pressure and the influence of alcohol. The lines between rape and sex begin to blur. The one-in-four statistic on those purple posters is measuring something elusive. It is measuring her word against his in a realm where words barely exist. There is a gray area in which one person's rape may be another's bad night. Definitions become entangled in passionate ideological battles. There hasn't been a remarkable change in the number of women being raped; just a change in how receptive the political climate is to those numbers.

The next question, then, is who is identifying this epidemic and why. Somebody is "finding" this rape crisis, and finding it for a reason. Asserting the prevalence of rape lends urgency, authority to a broader critique of culture.

In a dramatic description of the rape crisis, Naomi Wolf writes in *The Beauty Myth* that "Cultural representation of glamorized degradation has created a situation among the young in which boys rape and girls get raped *as a normal course of events.*" The italics are hers. Whether or not Wolf really believes rape is part of the "normal course of events" these days, she is making a larger point. Wolf's rhetorical excess serves her larger polemic about sexual politics. Her dramatic prose is a call to arms. She is trying to rally the feminist troops. Wolf uses rape as a red flag, an undeniable sign that things are falling apart.

From Susan Brownmiller—who brought the politics of rape into the mainstream with her 1975 best-seller, *Against Our Will: Men, Women and Rape*—to Naomi Wolf, feminist prophets of the rape crisis are talking about something more than forced penetration. They are talking about what they define as a "rape culture." Rape is a natural trump card for feminism. Arguments about rape can be used to sequester feminism in the teary province of trauma and crisis. By blocking analysis with its claims to unique pandemic suffering, the rape crisis becomes a powerful source of authority.

> *The so-called rape epidemic on campuses is . . . more about a change in sexual politics than a change in sexual behavior.*

Dead serious, eyes wide with concern, a college senior tells me that she believes one in four is too conservative an estimate. This is not the first time I've heard this. She tells me the right statistic is closer to one in two. That means one in two women are raped. It's amazing, she says, amazing that so many of us are sexually assaulted every day.

What is amazing is that this student actually believes that 50 percent of women are raped. This is the true crisis. Some substantial number of young women are walking around with this alarming belief: a hyperbole containing within it a state of perpetual fear.

"Acquaintance Rape: Is Dating Dangerous?" is a pamphlet commonly found at counseling centers. The cover title rises from the shards of a shattered photograph of a boy and girl dancing. Inside, the pamphlet offers a sample date-rape scenario. She thinks:

> He was really good looking and he had a great smile. . . . We talked and found we had a lot in common. I really liked him. When he asked me over to his place for a drink I thought it would be O.K. He was such a good listener and I wanted him to ask me out again.

She's just looking for a sensitive boy, a good listener with a nice smile, but unfortunately his intentions are not as pure as hers. Beneath that nice smile, he thinks:

> She looked really hot, wearing a sexy dress that showed off her great body. We started talking right away. I knew that she liked me by the way she kept smiling and touching my arm while she was speaking. She seemed pretty relaxed so I asked her back to my place for a drink. . . . When she said "Yes" I knew that I was going to be lucky!

These cardboard stereotypes don't just educate freshmen about rape. They also educate them about "dates" and about sexual desire. With titles like "Friends Raping Friends: Could It Happen to You?" date-rape pamphlets call into question all relationships between men and women. Beyond warning students about rape, the rape-crisis movement produces its own images of sexual behavior, in which men exert pressure and women resist. By defining the dangerous date in these terms—with this type of male and this type of female, and their different expectations—these pamphlets promote their own perspective on how men and women feel about sex: men are lascivious, women are innocent.

The sleek images of pressure and resistance projected in rape education movies, videotapes, pamphlets and speeches create a model of acceptable sexual behavior. The dont's imply their own set of do's. The movement against rape, then, not only dictates the way sex shouldn't be but also the way it should be. Sex should be gentle, it should not be aggressive; it should be absolutely equal, it should not involve domination and submission; it should be tender, not ambivalent; it should communicate respect, it shouldn't communicate consuming desire.

"Rape-crisis" feminism

In *Real Rape*, Susan Estrich, a professor of law at the University of Southern California Law Center, slips her ideas about the nature of sexual encounters into her legal analysis of the problem of rape. She writes:

> Many feminists would argue that so long as women are powerless relative to men, viewing a "yes" as a sign of true consent is misguided. . . . Many women who say yes to men they know, whether on dates or on the job, would say no if they could. . . . Women's silence sometimes is the product not of passion and desire but of pressure and fear.

Like Estrich, most rape-crisis feminists claim they are not talking about sex; they're talking about violence. But, like Estrich, they are also talking about sex. With their advice, their scenarios, their sample aggressive male, the message projects a clear comment on the nature of sexuality: women are often unwilling participants. They say yes because they feel they have to, because they are intimidated by male power.

The idea of "consent" has been redefined beyond the simple assertion that "no means no." Politically correct sex involves a yes, and a specific yes at that. According to the premise of "active consent," we can no longer afford ambiguity. We can no longer afford the dangers of unspoken consent. A former director of Columbia's date-rape education program told *New York* magazine, "Stone silence throughout an entire physical encounter with someone is not explicit consent."

This apparently practical, apparently clinical proscription cloaks retrograde assumptions about the way men and women experience sex. The idea that only an explicit yes means yes proposes that, like children, women have trouble communicating what they want. Beyond its dubious premise about the limits of female communication, the idea of active consent bolsters stereotypes of men just out to "get some" and women who don't really want any.

Rape-crisis feminists express nostalgia for the days of greater social control, when the university acted in loco parentis and women were protected from the insatiable force of male desire. The rhetoric of feminists and conservatives blurs and overlaps in this desire to keep our youth safe and pure.

By viewing rape as encompassing more than the use or threat of physical violence to coerce someone into sex, rape-crisis feminists reinforce traditional views about the fragility of the female body and will. Accord-

ing to common definitions of date rape, even "verbal coercion" or "manipulation" constitutes rape. Verbal coercion is defined as "a woman's
consenting to unwanted sexual activity because of a man's verbal arguments not including verbal threats of force." The belief that "verbal coercion" is rape pervades workshops, counseling sessions and student opinion pieces. The suggestion lurking beneath this definition of rape is that
men are not just physically but also intellectually and emotionally more
powerful than women.

Imagine men sitting around in a circle talking about how she called
him impotent and how she manipulated him into sex, how violated and
dirty he felt afterward, how coercive she was, how she got him drunk first,
how he hated his body and he couldn't eat for three weeks afterward.
Imagine him calling this rape. Everyone feels the weight of emotional
pressure at one time or another. The question is not whether people pressure each other but how our minds and our culture transform that pressure into full-blown assault. There would never be a rule or a law or even
a pamphlet or peer counseling group for men who claimed to have been
emotionally raped or verbally pressured into sex. And for the same reasons—assumption of basic competence, free will and strength of character—there should be no such rules or groups or pamphlets about women.

In discussing rape, campus feminists often slip into an outdated sexist vocabulary. But we have to be careful about using rape as metaphor.
The sheer physical fact of rape has always been loaded with cultural
meaning. Throughout history, women's bodies have been seen as property, as chaste objects, as virtuous vessels to be "dishonored," "ruined,"
"defiled." Their purity or lack of purity has been a measure of value for
the men to whom they belonged.

"Politically, I call it rape whenever a woman has sex and feels violated," writes Catharine MacKinnon, a law professor and feminist legal
scholar best known for her crusade against pornography. The language of
virtue and violation reinforces retrograde stereotypes. It backs women
into old corners. Younger feminists share MacKinnon's vocabulary and
the accompanying assumptions about women's bodies. In one student's
account of date rape in the *Rag*, a feminist magazine at Harvard, she talks
about the anguish of being "defiled." Another writes, "I long to be innocent again." With such anachronistic constructions of the female body,
with all their assumptions about female purity, these young women
frame their experience of rape in archaic, sexist terms. Of course, sophis-
ticated modern-day feminists don't use words like honor or virtue anymore. They know better than to say date-rape victims have been "defiled." Instead, they call it "post-traumatic stress syndrome." They tell the
victim she should not feel "shame," she should feel "traumatized."
Within their overtly political psychology, forced penetration takes on a
level of metaphysical significance: date rape resonates through a woman's
entire life.

*We all agree that rape is a terrible thing, but we no
longer agree on what rape is.*

Combating myths about rape is one of the central missions of the
rape-crisis movement. They spend money and energy trying to break

down myths like "She asked for it." But with all their noise about rape myths, rape-crisis feminists are generating their own. The plays, the poems, the pamphlets, the Take Back the Night speakouts, are propelled by the myth of innocence lost.

All the talk about empowering the voiceless dissolves into the image of the naive girl child who trusts the rakish man. This plot reaches back centuries. It propels Samuel Richardson's 18th-century epistolary novel, *Clarissa:* after hundreds of pages chronicling the minute details of her plight, her seduction and resistance, her break from her family, Clarissa is raped by the duplicitous Robert Lovelace. Afterward, she refuses to eat and fades toward a very virtuous, very religious death. Over a thousand pages are devoted to the story of her fall from innocence, a weighty event by 18th-century standards. But did these 20th-century girls, raised on Madonna videos and the 6 o'clock news, really trust that people were good until they themselves were raped? Maybe. Were these girls, raised on horror movies and glossy Hollywood sex scenes, really as innocent as all that? Maybe. But maybe the myth of lost innocence is a trope—convenient, appealing, politically effective.

Somebody is "finding" this rape crisis, and finding it for a reason.

As long as we're taking back the night, we might as well take back our own purity. Sure, we were all kind of innocent, playing in the sandbox with bright red shovels—boys, too. We can all look back through the tumultuous tunnel of adolescence on a honey-glazed childhood, with simple rules and early bedtimes. We don't have to look at parents fighting, at sibling struggles, at casting out one best friend for another in the Darwinian playground. This is not the innocence lost; this is the innocence we never had.

The idea of a fall from childhood grace, pinned on one particular moment, a moment over which we had no control, much lamented, gives our lives a compelling narrative structure. It's easy to see why the 17-year-old likes it; it's easy to see why the rape-crisis feminist likes it. It's a natural human impulse put to political purpose. But in generating and perpetuating such myths, we should keep in mind that myths about innocence have been used to keep women inside and behind veils. They have been used to keep them out of work and in labor.

It's not hard to imagine Clarissa, in jeans and a sweatshirt, transported into the 20th century, at a Take Back the Night march. She would speak for a long time about her deception and rape, about verbal coercion and anorexia, about her ensuing post-traumatic stress syndrome. Latter-day Clarissas may worry more about their "self esteem" than their virtue, but they are still attaching the same quasi-religious value to the physical act.

Calling It Rape, a play by Sonya Rasminsky, a recent Harvard graduate, is based on interviews with date-rape victims. The play, which has been performed at Harvard and may be taken into Boston-area high schools, begins with "To His Coy Mistress," by the 17th-century poet Andrew Marvell. Although generations of high-school and college students have read this as a romantic poem, a poem about desire and the struggle against mortality, Rasminsky has reinterpreted it as a poem about rape. "Had we but world enough, and time, this coyness, lady, were no crime." But what Andrew Marvell didn't know then, and we know now, is that the real crime is not her coyness but his verbal coercion.

Farther along, the actors recount a rape that hinges on misunderstanding. A boy and girl are watching videos and he starts to come on to her. She does not want to have sex. As the situation progresses, she says, in an oblique effort to communicate her lack of enthusiasm, "If you're going to [expletive] me, use a condom." He interprets that as a yes, but it's really a no. And, according to this play, what happens next, condom or no condom, is rape.

This is a central idea of the rape-crisis movement: that sex has become our tower of Babel. He doesn't know what she wants (not to have sex) and she doesn't know what he wants (to have sex)—until it's too late. He speaks boyspeak and she speaks girlspeak and what comes out of all this verbal chaos is a lot of rapes. The theory of mixed signals and crossed stars has to do with more than gender politics. It comes, in part, from the much-discussed diversity that has so radically shifted the social composition of the college class since the 50's.

Arguments about rape can be used to sequester feminism in the teary province of trauma and crisis.

Take my own Harvard dorm: the Adams House dining hall is large, with high ceilings and dark paneling. It hasn't changed much for generations. As soon as the students start milling around gathering salads, ice cream and coffee onto green trays, there are signs of change. There are students in jeans, flannel shirts, short skirts, girls in jackets, boys in bracelets, two pierced noses and lots of secondhand clothes.

Not so many years ago, this room was filled with boys in jackets and ties. Most of them were white, Christian and what we now call privileged. Students came from the same social milieu with the same social rules and it was assumed that everyone knew more or less how they were expected to behave with everyone else. Diversity and multiculturalism were unheard-of, and if they had been, they would have been dirty words. With the shift in college environments, with the introduction of black kids, Asian kids, Jewish kids, kids from the wrong side of the tracks of nearly every railroad in the country, there was an accompanying anxiety about how people behave. When ivory tower meets melting pot, it causes tension, some confusion, some need for readjustment. In explaining the need for intensive "orientation" programs, including workshops on date rape, Columbia's assistant dean for freshmen stated in an interview in the *New York Times:*

> You can't bring all these people together and say, "Now be one big happy community" without some sort of training. You can't just throw together somebody from a small town in Texas and someone from New York City and someone from a conservative fundamentalist home in the Midwest and say, "Now without any sort of conversation, be best friends and get along and respect one another."

Catharine Stimpson, a University Professor at Rutgers and longtime advocate of women's studies programs, once pointed out that it's sometimes easier for people to talk about gender than to talk about class. "Miscommunication" is in some sense a word for the friction between the way we were and the way we are. Just as the idea that we speak different languages is connected to gender—the arrival of women in classrooms, in dorms and in offices—it is also connected to class.

When the Southern heiress goes out with the plumber's son from the Bronx, when the kid from rural Arkansas goes out with a boy from Exeter, the anxiety is that they have different expectations. The dangerous "miscommunication" that recurs through the literature on date rape is a code word for difference in background. The rhetoric surrounding date rape and sexual harassment is in part a response to cultural mixing. The idea that men don't know what women mean when women say no stems from something deeper and more complicated than feminist concerns with rape.

What is rape?

People have asked me if I have ever been date-raped. And thinking back on complicated nights, on too many glasses of wine, on strange and familiar beds, I would have to say yes. With such a sweeping definition of rape, I wonder how many people there are, male or female, who haven't been date-raped at one point or another. People pressure and manipulate and cajole each other into all sorts of things all of the time. As Susan Sontag wrote, "Since Christianity upped the ante and concentrated on sexual behavior as the root of virtue, everything pertaining to sex has been a 'special case' in our culture, evoking peculiarly inconsistent attitudes." No human interactions are free from pressure, and the idea that sex is, or can be, makes it what Sontag calls a "special case," vulnerable to the inconsistent expectations of double standard.

With their expansive version of rape, rape-crisis feminists are inventing a kinder, gentler sexuality. Beneath the broad definition of rape, these feminists are endorsing their own utopian vision of sexual relations: sex without struggle, sex without power, sex without persuasion, sex without pursuit. If verbal coercion constitutes rape, then the word rape itself expands to include any kind of sex a woman experiences as negative.

When Martin Amis spoke at Princeton, he included a controversial joke: "As far as I'm concerned, you can change your mind before, even during, but just not after sex." The reason this joke is funny, and the reason it's also too serious to be funny, is that in the current atmosphere you can change your mind afterward. Regret can signify rape. A night that was a blur, a night you wish hadn't happened, can be rape. Since "verbal coercion" and "manipulation" are ambiguous, it's easy to decide afterwards that he manipulated you. You can realize it weeks or even years later. This is a movement that deals in retrospective trauma.

Rape has become a catchall expression, a word used to define everything that is unpleasant and disturbing about relations between the sexes. Students say things like "I realize that sexual harassment is a kind of rape." If we refer to a whole range of behavior from emotional pressure to sexual harassment as "rape," then the idea itself gets diluted. It ceases to be powerful as either description or accusation.

Some feminists actually collapse the distinction between rape and sex. Catharine MacKinnon writes:

> Compare victims' reports of rape with women's reports of sex. They look a lot alike. . . . In this light, the major distinction between intercourse (normal) and rape (abnormal) is that the normal

happens so often that one cannot get anyone to see anything wrong with it.

There are a few feminists involved in rape education who object to the current expanding definitions of sexual assault. Gillian Greensite, founder of the rape prevention education program at the University of California at Santa Cruz, writes that the seriousness of the crime "is being undermined by the growing tendency of some feminists to label all heterosexual miscommunication and insensitivity as acquaintance rape." From within the rape-crisis movement, Greensite's dissent makes an important point. If we are going to maintain an *idea* of rape, then we need to reserve it for instances of physical violence, or the threat of physical violence.

But some people want the melodrama. They want the absolute value placed on experience by absolute words. Words like "rape" and "verbal coercion" channel the confusing flow of experience into something easy to understand. The idea of date rape comes at us fast and coherent. It comes at us when we've just left home and haven't yet figured out where to put our new futons or how to organize our new social lives. The rhetoric about date rape defines the terms, gives names to nameless confusions and sorts through mixed feelings with a sort of insistent consistency. In the first rush of sexual experience, the fear of date rape offers a tangible framework to locate fears that are essentially abstract.

When my 55-year-old mother was young, navigating her way through dates, there was a definite social compass. There were places not to let him put his hands. There were invisible lines. The pill wasn't available. Abortion wasn't legal. And sex was just wrong. Her mother gave her "mad money" to take out on dates in case her date got drunk and she needed to escape. She had to go far enough to hold his interest and not far enough to endanger her reputation.

Now the rape-crisis feminists are offering new rules. They are giving a new political weight to the same old no. My mother's mother told her to drink sloe gin fizzes so she wouldn't drink too much and get too drunk and go too far. Now the date rape pamphlets tell us: "Avoid excessive use of alcohol and drugs. Alcohol and drugs interfere with clear thinking and effective communication." My mother's mother told her to stay away from empty rooms and dimly lighted streets. In *I Never Called It Rape*, Robin Warshaw writes, "Especially with recent acquaintances, women should insist on going only to public places such as restaurants and movie theaters."

The idea that only an explicit yes means yes proposes that, like children, women have trouble communicating what they want.

There is a danger in these new rules. We shouldn't need to be reminded that the rigidly conformist 50's were not the heyday of women's power. Barbara Ehrenreich writes of "re-making love," but there is a danger in remaking love in its old image. The terms may have changed, but attitudes about sex and women's bodies have not. Rape-crisis feminists threaten the progress that's been made. They are chasing the same stereotypes our mothers spent so much energy escaping.

One day I was looking through my mother's bookshelves and I found her old battered copy of Germaine Greer's feminist classic, *The Female Eunuch*. The pages were dogeared and whole passages marked with penciled notes. It was 1971 when Germaine Greer fanned the fires with *The Female Eunuch* and it was 1971 when my mother read it, brand new, explosive, a tough and sexy terrorism for the early stirrings of the feminist movement.

Today's rape-crisis feminists threaten to create their own version of the desexualized woman Greer complained of 20 years ago. Her comments need to be recycled for present-day feminism. "It is often falsely assumed," Greer writes,

> even by feminists, that sexuality is the enemy of the female who really wants to develop these aspects of her personality. . . . It was not the insistence upon her sex that weakened the American woman student's desire to make something of her education, but the insistence upon a *passive* sexual *role* [Greer's italics]. In fact, the chief instrument in the deflection and perversion of female energy is the denial of female sexuality for the substitution of femininity or sexlessness.

It is the passive sexual role that threatens us still, and it is the denial of female sexual agency that threatens to propel us backward.

9

An Alternative
View of Rape

Adele M. Stan

Adele M. Stan is a writer.

Females should feel free to direct both verbal epithets and physical force at males as a means of negatively reinforcing offensive behavior. By thus claiming their own power, women will be rebuffing the too-narrow definition of rape tendered by revisionist feminists such as Katie Roiphe and the notion that women are powerless often implied by protectionist feminists such as Andrea Dworkin and Catharine MacKinnon.

Were it not for an event in my own life I might view the current debate over date rape and the rape crisis movement with detached amusement, the way one does whenever opposing pockets of the intellectual elite have a go at each other. But for me the issue runs far deeper than that and it seems to me that neither side has really got it right.

In 1978 I was raped by an acquaintance in my college dorm room. This was no murky instance of date rape; I was asleep when the perpetrator, a guest at a party my roommate was giving in our campus apartment, let himself in, gripped my arms over my head and bored his way into me.

Of course I protested, but I was afraid to do so too loudly, for just outside the door lurked the beer-soaked players of an entire hockey team, and I had heard too many boasts from athletes about girls who had "pulled the train" for a team, who had serviced 10 or 15 members in a single night. So I resigned myself to my fate, taking the advice of police experts on violent crime against women: "Resistance only excites them."

Today's debate is fueled in part by Katie Roiphe's book *The Morning After: Sex, Fear and Feminism on Campus*, which argues that young women are being whipped by feminists into a frenzy of fear about a rape crisis that doesn't exist.

Revisionists like Ms. Roiphe often point out that some women are categorized as rape victims in studies even though they do not identify themselves as such. But if you asked me, even several years after my dorm-room horror, if I had ever been raped, I doubt I would have said yes. It was years before I told *anyone* about the assault; the experience was too painful and the guilt at not having resisted harder was overwhelming. Revisionists who believe they would have been more forthcoming could at least show a little gratitude to the women's movement for their untroubled psyches.

On the other side are the protectionist feminists, those so focused on shielding women from harm that they inadvertently encourage us to exalt our status as victims. In their advocacy for anti-pornography legislation, Catharine MacKinnon and Andrea Dworkin often refer to the powerlessness of women as if it were innate.

I resist the notion of women as sexually pure damsels in need of special protections. In the 1980's, when I was working at *Ms.* magazine, I heard an editor express concern about her politically incorrect sexual fantasies, and was shocked by the puritanism I saw creeping into the women's movement. More concerned with reality than fantasy, I came to this movement for sexual equity, not sexual purity.

I resist the notion of women as sexually pure
damsels in need of special protections.

The revisionists and the protectionists each cling to one or another clause of the old social contract between the sexes. Though Katie Roiphe acknowledges the widespread problem of sexual harassment, and she rightly insists that we are each responsible for our own actions (e.g., having sex with someone because you're tipsy doesn't mean he raped you), she implies that nearly any level of aggression visited upon us, short of stranger-rape at knifepoint, is no big deal.

On the other hand, what are we to make of Andrea Dworkin's statement that women's silence over the dangers we face at the hands of men is "that silence into which we are born because we are women"?

I reject both assumptions. Since being raped, a remarkable thing happened to me—I became violent, and in this violence found liberation. I have been grabbed several times by strangers on the street, and I never let the culprit go without physically attacking him. When a vile remark is shouted at me, I shout back something equally vile.

Yet feminists often discourage women from such behavior. *Newsday* ran a front-page article on a woman who wielded a kitchen knife to foil a would-be rapist who broke into her apartment. The next day, a number of experts, including the sex crimes prosecutor Linda Fairstein, cautioned readers not to try the same thing—you could get killed. Isn't it time we applauded women who defend themselves against attack? Why assume that women don't have the judgment to assess their chances of success?

Proper nurturance

Likewise, we must reconsider how we raise our children. I believe that the pattern of sexual harassment that begins in grade school could be altered if we taught our daughters to fight back when attacked by boys. We expect girls to be comforted with the admonition not to pay them any mind; boys are like that. In other words: get used to it.

If more boys received more negative reinforcement at the hands of girls, the offensive behavior might be discouraged. At the very least, girls would feel less powerless. If there really is a war against women, then we ought to be raising women warriors.

Until all feminists are willing to rethink the social contract—including the provisions that cede our well-being to the goodwill of men and that proclaim us to be, like cows, one of nature's mute and gentle creations—we will be left to the task of laying blame when we could be seeking real solutions.

10

Student-Professor Sexual Relations: A Forum Discussion

Jack Hitt, Joan Blythe, John Boswell, Leon Botstein, and William Kerrigan

Harper's Magazine contributing editor Jack Hitt moderated this forum discussion among educators Joan Blythe, John Boswell, Leon Botstein, and William Kerrigan.

Regulations proscribing student-professor romances have increased greatly in the last few years (over two dozen colleges have formally declared such relationships illicit). A forum on the subject of student-professor sexual relations was organized by *Harper's Magazine*. Moderated by Jack Hitt, a contributing editor of *Harper's*, four distinguished college educators expressed their views on this perennially controversial topic. While opinions on specific areas of the subject often varied both in degree and substance, the majority of panelists stressed the positive aspects of student-professor romantic ties.

The following forum is based on a discussion held over dinner at the Terrace, a restaurant on the campus of Columbia University, in New York City. Jack Hitt served as moderator.

JACK HITT is a contributing editor of *Harper's Magazine*. He has just completed a book on the medieval road to Santiago, Spain, to be published by Poseidon Press.

JOAN BLYTHE is an associate professor of English at the University of Kentucky. She is a scholar of medieval and Renaissance literature and is currently completing a book entitled *The Sin of the Tongue*.

JOHN BOSWELL is the A. Whitney Griswold Professor of History at Yale University. He is the author of *Christianity, Social Tolerance, and Homosexuality* and is currently at work on *An Unhappy Family: The Interaction of Judaism, Christianity, and Islam in the Medieval Mediterranean*.

LEON BOTSTEIN is the president of Bard College and the music director of the American Symphony Orchestra. He is the author of *Judentum und*

Modernität, published by Boehlau in Vienna, which will appear in English translation, published by Yale University Press, in 1994.

WILLIAM KERRIGAN is a professor of English and the director of the Program on Psychoanalytic Studies at the University of Massachusetts (Amherst). His most recent book, *Hamlet's Perfection*, was published in 1993 by Johns Hopkins University Press.

I. Why now?

JACK HITT: Students returning to campuses around the country this fall will be resuming a conversation I cannot imagine unfolding ten or twenty years ago—a debate about whether formal bans should be adopted on some or all student-professor sexual relationships. How did we get here?

JOHN BOSWELL: These bans are very much a result of the rootlessness that is prevalent among the students arriving on campus. In times of social disruption, people tend to rely on institutions and laws to replace more private and traditional mechanisms for maintaining order. This shift is backed up by the widespread belief that American eighteen-year-olds should not be tainted with sexuality. But these are not children we are talking about. In fact, they are at a point in their lives when they are really exploring their erotic feelings.

JOAN BLYTHE: One supposition is that freshmen are naive eighteen-year-olds who need protecting. Another is that the university experience can be reduced to a business deal: students pay money, hear lectures, get diplomas, and are provided a secure place in an increasingly troubled economy. An experience that was once one of transformation is now more commonly thought of as a *transaction*—a predictable product for money paid.

WILLIAM KERRIGAN: It's the consumer approach to education. It says: Yes, I want higher education. But I want a warranty that nothing formative, vital, or transformative will happen to me. In particular, should one of my teachers initiate a sexual moment of sufficient power to upset me, I reserve the right to destroy his career.

LEON BOTSTEIN: Let's give the supporters of a ban their due. There *is* a power differential in the relationship between a student and his or her teacher. And a sexual relationship between a teacher and a student is, in fact, at odds with the task of teaching. Before we start nailing our opponents as puritans, hypocrites, or idiots, let's realize that we're dealing in murky definitions that could cause problems in the conduct of teacher-student relationships.

KERRIGAN: This debate forces those, like myself, who abhor the notion of a ban to say things that used to go without saying. Prudery is a great offense against life. Without a sex act, none of us would be here. And whenever civilization sets out a law against a sexual practice or expression, it invariably produces a desire to break that law. That's the way eroticism works.

HITT: Then wouldn't a ban be good? Wouldn't legislation create new and exciting taboos?

KERRIGAN: There already is a connection between student-faculty sex and what Freud called the supreme taboo—the incest taboo. Teachers are like parents—*in loco parentis*—but because we're not parents there is no obvious sexual revulsion that prevents relations with students. What

Who wrote the (rule) book of love?

University	Date of policy	Policy	Punishment
College of William and Mary	June 1991	"Faculty members are advised against participating in amorous relationships with students enrolled in their classes or with students whom they . . . evaluate, grade, or supervise." If a professor does become involved with his or her student, "the faculty member shall report the situation promptly and seek advice and counsel from an appropriate administrative superior."	"Members of the university community who believe themselves to be affected adversely by violation of this policy may initiate a complaint with the appropriate dean." No specific sanctions.
Tufts University	January 1, 1992	"It is a violation of University policy if a faculty member . . . engages in an amorous, dating, or sexual relationship with a student whom he/she instructs, evaluates, supervises, advises. Voluntary consent by the student . . . is suspect."	"Disciplinary action."
Indiana University	June 1992	"All amorous or sexual relationships between faculty members and students are unacceptable when the faculty member has professional responsibility for the student. . . . Voluntary consent by the student in such a relationship is suspect, given the fundamental asymmetric nature of the relationship."	No specific sanctions.
Harvard and Radcliffe Colleges	September 1992	"Officers and other members of the teaching staff should be aware that any romantic involvement with their students makes them liable for formal action against them. . . . Amorous relationships between members of the Faculty and students that occur outside the instructional context can also lead to difficulties."	No specific sanctions.
Amherst College	March 2, 1993	"The College does not condone, and in fact strongly discourages, consensual relationships between faculty members and students. . . . The College requires a faculty member to remove himself or herself form any supervisory, evaluative, advisory, or other pedagogical role involving the student with whom he or she has had or currently has a sexual relationship."	Sanctions are being reviewed.
Oberlin College	June 1993	"It is unwise for faculty members to engage in sexual relationships with students even when both parties have consented to the relationship. . . . Relations are prohibited when a student is enrolled in a class taught by the faculty member."	"Offenses involving abuse of power, as opposed to misconduct between equals, and especially repeated abuses of power are always severe and may result in dismissal."
Stanford University	Expected fall 1993	"Relationships may undermine the real or perceived integrity of the supervision and evaluation provided, particularly the trust inherent in the student-faculty relationship."	None.

You're a college administrator. For the past semester, your campus has been embroiled in a heated debate over faculty-student sex, a debate filled with arguments about rights, victims, abuse, and heartbreak. Now comes the hard part: actually formulating the ban. How do you shrink the vicissitudes of the heart into the language of the academic-policy manual? Above, some attempts to do just that.

we're creating with these bans are not taboos but punishments.

BOTSTEIN: It's important to grasp that the context in which this student-teacher issue is couched is a political debate in the United States that is, in general, an impoverished one. People are reluctant to really debate political issues. Sexuality has become a substitute for politics. There's been an erosion of the political interchange. Look at the presidential election. We're more interested in Clinton's sex life than his politics. Sexuality has *become* America's politics, and the university is a victim of the dissolution between matters private and public.

KERRIGAN: I happen to think that the debate over this issue *is* a real political discussion. Alcibiades in Athens, Nero in Rome—such issues have always been part of the political debate, just as sexuality has always been a part of education. The university is not a sex-free environment. Nor is the classroom.

BLYTHE: The political debate today, on campus and off, is about identity. And sexual identity—which includes whom you have relationships with and under what terms—is among the most fundamental of issues being debated.

II. The education of a virgin

HITT: To hear those supporting a ban on student-professor relationships, you'd think there were suddenly hundreds of teachers on every campus who are sleeping with their students. But this isn't the case. What kind of phenomenon are we talking about here?

KERRIGAN: I have been the subject of advances from male and female students for twenty-five years. I've had them come at me right and left. I've had people take their clothes off in my office. And there is a particular kind of student I have responded to. I am not defending Don Juanism, you know, sex for grades and so forth. But there is a kind of student I've come across in my career who was working through something that only a professor could help her with. I'm talking about a female student who, for one reason or another, has unnaturally prolonged her virginity. Maybe there's a strong father, maybe there's a religious background. And if she loses that virginity with a man who is not a teacher, she's going to marry that man, boom. And I don't think the marriage is going to be very good.

There have been times when this virginity has been presented to me as something that I, not quite another man, half an authority figure, can handle—a thing whose preciousness I realize. These relationships, like all relationships, are hard to describe, and certainly difficult to defend in today's environment. Like all human relationships, they are flawed and sometimes tragic. There usually is this initial idealism—the teacher presents ideas in a beautiful form, and so there is this element of seduction in pedagogy. And then things come down to earth, and there often follows disappointment and, on the part of the student, anger. But still, these relationships exist between adults and can be quite beautiful and genuinely transforming. It's very powerful sexually and psychologically, and because of that power, one can touch a student in a positive way. So if you want to oppose the imposition of this ban, I say, let's get honest and describe positive instances of sex between students and faculty.

BOTSTEIN: What comes to my mind is, one, a sense of relief that you're not on the faculty at my college. And two, I'm not certain anyone wants to make a virtue of a private act.

BOSWELL: But what these bans do is conflate the public and private realms. Should we allow the public to interfere in what is essentially a private issue?

BOTSTEIN: I agree, there should be no bans. I am against them. But I share the implicit *ideology* of the bans. What I disagree with is their political entrance into the public arena.

KERRIGAN: I *do* disagree with their ideology. Sometimes these affairs last a week, and they're gone. Sometimes a semester or two. Sometimes they grow into things of great constancy, such as, I may as well reveal, my own marriage. Are you saying you want a generation in which no marriages or affairs result from student-teacher relationships?

BOTSTEIN: I favor a voluntary system, something on the order of a Hippocratic oath. You internalize enough of what people expect so that intelligent, responsible people can make judgments and discriminations by circumstance and event.

BOSWELL: I agree. There are already harassment procedures at most schools.

BLYTHE: And students are glad of that, but they think the bans are ludicrous. I asked my sophomore Western Lit survey class and my Milton seminar about this ban. One girl said, "I'd see how many professors I could screw that week." For others it was an idea they had never entertained and suddenly they were saying, "Hmm, my professor . . ." It's like medieval penitential manuals. In confessing parishioners, priests were warned against bringing up sins not yet committed by asking questions like, Did you give your neighbor's husband a blow job? Maybe she just hadn't thought of it yet.

Let's get honest and describe positive instances of sex between students and faculty.

BOSWELL: I don't think the problem is putting sex with professors in the students' minds. Like William, I have students absolutely throw themselves at me. I had this incredibly attractive jock come to my office when eighty students were applying for fifteen seats in a class. So I had them all turn in a written statement signed only by their last name. I didn't even want to know their gender. So he came to my office after hours wearing nothing but a pair of gym shorts. Not even shoes. I looked him up and down. And he said, "Professor Boswell, is there something else I can do to get into your class?" And I said, "No, I think you've done all you decently can."

BLYTHE: Did he get in?

BOSWELL: No. But had I given in to temptation, imagine the complications and necessary subterfuges I would have invited. I think self-restraint is the way to avoid being unfair.

BOTSTEIN: The most important element of a university is honesty. What I don't like about an overt ban is that it forces people to lie. When you make legislation that can't be enforced in human communities, you undermine the law. And on the campus, this distorts the fundamental integrity of the university, which is self-regulation and respect for truth. Instead of admitting that something went wrong, the student acts as we do on the outside. We lie—and hire lawyers to get us off. We deny—and put our hope in an adversarial proceeding in which the best defense wins. Our stand at the academy should be different. It ought to be about proof and truth and a sensible notion of fact and fiction. What we're teaching these young people with these adjudications is that those who admit they were drunk or they did something wrong and deal with it openly are *fools*.

III. Who's fighting the fight?

HITT: Why does this ban seem largely to concern young women and their virtue? I thought that traditionally the great fear was of homosexual student-teacher relations.

BOSWELL: It is true that the ban is being promoted by feminists, but the homosexual subtext is there. In fact, in a society that did not have this horror of young boys being seduced, I doubt you would see the kind of support you do for the kind of ban we're talking about. Many, many Americans fear homosexuality. People out there are paranoid about gay men coming on to their sons.

BLYTHE: On campuses, where the battle is being waged, homosexuality is not the central issue, because the people proposing these bans are heterosexual and this debate is really about *their* private lives. About what they fear in themselves, their own relationships and their own desire. The people who voice these concerns are precisely those who desire the eighteen-year-old. These codes have to do with protecting the most privileged of American students. This is not a debate burning at the community-college level. Those pushing for a ban are people who fear real life, especially the protean power of lust. College for them is about *isolation* from the real world, not an introduction to it.

KERRIGAN: This is a case where the left and the right are in bed together.

BOTSTEIN: That's right, although "left" and "right" aren't great words. The alliance focuses on the power relationship between men and women in the academy. The majority of faculty members are male, and this ban uses the paradigm of male faculty and female student to reveal the abuse of male-dominated—

KERRIGAN: The "paradigm" is a generation of academic feminists who push this legislation because in an era when a leer constitutes rape, they believe they are powerful enough to punish womanizing male colleagues.

BOSWELL: Why are they so disturbed? Is this simply one of the few areas they can regulate?

BOTSTEIN: Well, I do think there's a history here. To give the other side some due, a fair amount of data shows a long tradition of abuse. Graduate students may be the worst-treated creatures, reduced to servility, and if sexuality's a part, then—

BLYTHE: It also may be the most pleasant part of graduate school.

BOTSTEIN: Well, you're assuming something about the quality of the sexual exchange that I don't want to comment on. But let's not be unfair. I've had enough encounters with parents who are not bizarre or crazy, and they are concerned.

BLYTHE: What age student are you talking about?

BOTSTEIN: Between eighteen and twenty-one.

BLYTHE: Most students at eighteen know more about sex than their own parents.

KERRIGAN: Exactly. Who are these women? Are they all like Anita Hill, who, you'll remember, testified that she had to check into a hospital with stomach ailments after hearing from Clarence Thomas an account of a Long Dong Silver movie?

BOTSTEIN: Don't trivialize the critic, please.

HITT: Is there some larger agenda or motive behind these bans?

BLYTHE: Yes. The force that is pushing for these bans is abetted by an administration whose agenda includes castration of the humanities.

BOTSTEIN: That's absurd. The administrators haven't sought out this problem. If anything, they've ducked it. They've run for the hills, fearful of litigation, suits seeking financial damages, and so on. They have simply been forced into this arena, kicking and screaming, by a divisive faculty debate.

BLYTHE: It's a simple fact that these romances are most often found in the humanities. Since the administration is biased against any unprofitable part of the university—especially those that can't attract fat research grants—it's no coincidence that administrators have chosen to jump on this issue.

KERRIGAN: But in the faculty, who's behind this? By and large, feminists.

BOTSTEIN: They may be people who have a real concern about victimization. They may be authentic puritans; still, I respect such people.

BLYTHE: Except they're *not* puritans. They think non-marital sex is fine, as long as they can control it.

BOTSTEIN: Now, wait. Let's get straight what the proponents of the ban are arguing. They're not arguing the absence of sexuality.

BLYTHE: They are arguing the abdication of responsibility by an individual for her or his own actions.

BOTSTEIN: No, they're not. They are suggesting that in the relationship of student and teacher, restraint be exercised.

IV. The obligations of intercourse

BOTSTEIN: Do we share some residual partial allegiance to the idea that passion and reason are in some sense at odds?

BLYTHE: No.

KERRIGAN: No, sir.

BOTSTEIN: I assumed as much. I think part of the ban rests on the assumption that there's something dispassionate about the conduct of reason that passion interrupts. It's an eighteenth-century construct of the human personality.

BOSWELL: The relationship is not antipodal, but it is complicated.

KERRIGAN: The problem with the reason/passion division is the assumption that reason recognizes complexity and ambiguity and that passion is this animalistic thing that merely takes possession. Now, I know Norman Mailer is very out of fashion today, but one thing he taught me when I was twenty years old is that good sex is fabulously complicated, in the way that a great poem is complicated. This is not a matter of mindless passion versus complex philosophy.

BOTSTEIN: Let me say this: I think sexual relations trigger a set of ethical obligations.

BLYTHE: Ethical obligations?

BOTSTEIN: Ethical obligations.

KERRIGAN: *Ethical* obligations?

BOTSTEIN: Allow me to approach it this way. I am partisan, out of obligation, to my parents, my spouse, my children, and other members of my family in a way that overrides fairness. I will stop at nothing to advance them. If I am a judge in a violin competition and my grandmother enters, my opinion would be slanted toward her from the start, no matter what. That's why judges disqualify themselves. Now, I happen to think that when, as a teacher, you go beyond flirtation with a student, you trigger a set of ethical obligations that override the desire to be fair. I happen to think, as well, that the process of teaching is a process of the adjudication of fairness. So my conclusion is that when you are having sexual relations with one of your students, you are in this sense being unfair to the others.

BOSWELL: A way to solve that problem is disclosure. A colleague of mine who married his graduate student and continues to write her recommendations should begin his letters, "My wife . . ."

BLYTHE: I totally disagree. No judgment is purely musical or purely literary—purely objective as to merit. It's always subjective.

BOSWELL: You don't think people should aspire to be fair?

BLYTHE: I think people should aspire to be great. I would hope if your grandmother were the best violinist out there, you would give her the award.

BOTSTEIN: What if my grandmother were not the best violinist?

BLYTHE: Then you *wouldn't* give her the award. See how it works?

KERRIGAN: What's tiresome about what you've been saying, Leon, is the assumption that we have this Kantian moral sense, a system of absolutes that we must either abide by or recede into corruption. You assume that when you sleep with someone, you gain these obligations that override other intellectual perceptions. I wouldn't describe it that way. If you're asked to compare your beloved's talent to that of three others in a contest, you'll get disillusioned pretty quickly. In the end, you may be in the best position of all to make the judgment or write a letter of recommendation.

V. Secular Pentecostalism

HITT: How is the campus changing? People in their late thirties and forties say that for them, college was a time to try on new identities, be fitted with a radical idea or two, and experiment in many ways. Nowadays, this line of thinking goes, college is about upwardly adjusting one's résumé.

BOTSTEIN: Nostalgia. In the twenty-two years I've been involved with colleges, there hasn't been any appreciable change in idealism. It's the fraudulent nostalgia of aging people who look back on their college youth and say, "When I went to college . . ." Nonsense, wrong.

What *has* changed is the sense of informality in the American university. What's been lost is the sense of comfort people had with an informal relationship between students and faculty. And this involves taking a drink, smoking, and all forms of informality that might result in an accusation of "I have been victimized." So you restrict your behavior until it's "beyond reproach," and what you've lost—

KERRIGAN: Are the rough edges of human beings.

BOTSTEIN: Remember *Chariots of Fire*? It may have been a bit romanticized, but it showed an Oxford common room where professors offered undergraduates sherry. That's against the law today. Not possible. Forbidden. A certain sensibility has driven out conviviality.

BLYTHE: Where I'm from, we call it Pentecostalism—a desire to have the truth set in stone, Moses-style. This sensibility yearns for sound doctrine that doesn't change, is expressed in absolutes, and against which is set a tasty array of penalties. Pentecostalism has an element of the fascist to it.

BOTSTEIN: I agree.

BLYTHE: Pentecostalism is pyramidal, hierarchical, and looks to a father figure to tell us what to do. It has no sense of history. Pentecostalism shuns ambiguity and distrusts any statement that can't be fashioned into a simple certainty. On the most practical level, take course evaluations: Once upon a time, students were asked, "What did you get out of this course?" Today they are asked, on a standardized sheet, "How effective is the instructor?" with the options—"Excellent?" "Good?" "Average?" "Below Average?" "Poor?"—in bubbles to be blackened in with a No. 2 lead pencil.

BOTSTEIN: In my experience, a recurrent complaint among students is that they had hoped for more informality with professors. Instead, campus life seems more impersonal, "cut and dried," if you will.

HITT: Is the loss of informality a matter of a new and increasingly heterogeneous population showing up on campus? In a way, American colleges have promoted diversity as a theory for generations, but only recently has true diversity finally arrived on campus. Maybe it has everyone nervous.

BOTSTEIN: I don't think it's that much more diverse.

BOSWELL: Maybe not. But the expression of that diversity is different. Calvin Trillin's new book, *Remembering Denny*, is about how his generation repressed many of their differences to present a kind of homogeneity, which was achieved then at the price of many people pretending to be someone they were not. Today, that's no longer the case.

BOTSTEIN: This shift turns the idea of the traditional university inside out. In the Middle Ages, the university sought to be a place that was immune from the severity of civil jurisdiction. There was to be a spirit of liberty and self-regulation—hence fraternities and other such developments. Now the rules the universities promulgate are more ferocious than those found in civil society. Consider the category of date rape.

KERRIGAN: Or offensive speech. The standards are comically higher.

What comes to my mind is . . . a sense of relief that you're not on the faculty at my college.

HITT: Couldn't it be that these kids are begging for rules? Given the campus's diversity—or the heightened expression of differences—could one assume that these kids are anxious and confused about what the common code of behavior is? So they cry out for rules, look to their smart professors for help, but find instead a bunch of liberals who get the willies around "rules."

BOSWELL: You're right, but our reply is, and rightly so, "Tough. We can't make life simple for you. You must think for yourselves." Getting across this message has always been the university's ultimate mission.

BLYTHE: And look at what gets preserved by such rules—a desiccated sexuality. Narrow and pinched, it assumes that sex is merely an act of physical engineering, some kind of biological insertion. Sexuality is not a simple act but the very air we breathe. People can have orgasms sitting in a class listening to a good lecturer. Why are we defining sexuality so narrowly? It's a university. The air is alive with sexuality without anyone touching. When these proponents of a student-professor sex ban talk about sexuality, they mean only something harmful. They are not talking about desire, about eros. Education is a kind of desire, the desire to learn. You cannot rein it in with the blunt instrument of a policy manual.

VI. The lyricism of a pat on the ass

HITT: Couldn't all this confusion on campus be an argument—a kind of conversation—among disparate groups as they struggle to create a new etiquette, a new common culture with simple table manners and dating rituals for a complex mosaic of people?

BLYTHE: And the only common language among these groups is sexuality. It's the only common language we have.

HITT: Then it makes sense that sexuality is the arena where such a conversation would take place, no?

BLYTHE: Precisely. Everyone's got a sexuality, and everyone's most fundamental identity is tied up with it. It's your history, your first history, and the most interesting history. Each of us is a series of transformations related to sexuality, whether it's ex-wives, boyfriends, girlfriends, husbands, or charged glands in the library.

BOTSTEIN: That seems to be the least interesting history to me, frankly.

BLYTHE: We no longer have a religious common ground, a shared cultural background.

HITT: Therefore, sexuality is the common crucible in which a new etiquette for a more diverse culture is forged. Maybe the only thing we have in common, at long last, are our genitals.

BOTSTEIN: I'm getting very depressed.

KERRIGAN: You know, I recently had a serious philosophical debate with a graduate student. Tell me, which is the truer expression of desire for a male toward a female: writing her a sonnet or patting her on the ass?

BOTSTEIN: It depends on whether the person can write.

HITT: And, therefore, does it also depend on the quality of the ass?

BOTSTEIN: Actually, for me it would be a really committed performance in music, without words. That would be the highest expression in this higher range of discussion of sexuality. That's as close as I can get to the creative power.

KERRIGAN: I ask the question because it reveals something about etiquette. A pat on the ass in, say, a redneck bar is not decried as rape but fits into a friendly culture that allows a man or a woman to say, "I like you. I want to touch you." A pat on the ass nowadays is an interesting problem. One pat and you're a lout; more than one, and you are Bob Packwood, hauled to the stockades, buried in lawsuits.

BOTSTEIN: I find it all offensive. Call me a puritan. I think a pat on the ass is offensive.

KERRIGAN: Really? There's something wrong about a hand and an ass coming into contact?

BOTSTEIN: Without consent. There's the issue of consent.

KERRIGAN: *Without* consent. Imagine it.

BOTSTEIN: Without consent, it's offensive. I am not in favor of it.

BOSWELL: Baseball players can get away with this. But if you just did it to a strange man on the subway, he'd punch you in the nose, and I think you'd deserve it.

HITT: I guess I have trouble, too, William. A pat on the ass at the first meeting? I don't know.

KERRIGAN: Fifth or sixth encounter?

HITT: Well, okay, probably.

KERRIGAN: See, following the track of this conversation, you wind up making any pass at a woman into something offensive. Now, flirtation is a matter of etiquette, etc. But it's a wretched culture indeed that can't make room for flirtation—some way for one soul to tell another, "I want to touch you."

BOSWELL: Both of you may be right, in that Leon says that etiquette should be observed because it is convention and William is saying that convention can be changed with consideration for human feeling. And yet, William, even though we can change the way we eat, that doesn't mean we can ask people to throw food on the floor and have them gobble it down there.

VII. A nostalgia for the stockade

BOTSTEIN: It's interesting. I would argue that students through the 1960s accepted the idea that higher education was about trying on the clothes of adulthood, so they eagerly accepted responsibility for their actions. If they got involved with someone, if they got drunk, if they hurt someone, they sought to take responsibility. Today's students believe they are not responsible; quite the opposite, they feel they are *owed* something—an entitlement to a reward from distress. And when they are hurt, they are more prone to call themselves "victims." Life, as the theologians have taught us for a long time, is inherently victimizing. So when something goes wrong, a student feels empowered to distribute the blame elsewhere. Let's say a relationship between a student and professor goes sour, for whatever reason.

KERRIGAN: It's bound to.

BOTSTEIN: Rather than say, "This is my life, I take responsibility," the reaction today is, "I have suffered, I wish to be entitled to some reparation." And where the puritan character really comes out is in the desire for punishment, a public flogging of a presumed wrongdoer. The ban proponents believe that punishment has a psychic benefit. They want to put the malefactor in stockades and force him to feel the heat of public humiliation. So the final message of higher education becomes not, as John said, "Life is tough, unfair, tricky, difficult, complex; ergo, learn to take responsibility and live with it," but "All problems in your life can be reduced to the task of exacting redress."

BOSWELL: People don't have the attitude "Well, it's rotten, let's make it better," but "I've suffered, so give me my fifteen minutes of fame."

BOTSTEIN: Or "I feel guilty about my participation in what went wrong. I wish to displace my guilt by focusing on somebody who did it to me." It's a disavowal of responsibility.

BLYTHE: We've spoken about the ill effect these bans have on students. But we forget ourselves, the teachers. Education is also a transformation of us by our students, allowing us to learn and be changed by the encounter of a classroom. This ban is a prophylactic to that kind of fertility as well. It erects a barrier because it presents me, the teacher, as rapacious, predatory, and dangerous even before I walk into the classroom.

BOTSTEIN: But does it take a consummation of the sexual dimension to be transformed?

BLYTHE: Of course not. But in setting up a law, you have immediately cast me as a potential raptor. You are emphasizing my role not as educator but as assailant. You define me in negative terms, stripping me of my ability to teach.

BOTSTEIN: This is interesting. You're saying that by writing the law, you are instantly identified as a potential predator?

BLYTHE: Yes. This discussion turns on one of the seven deadly sins—lust, specifically between a professor and a student. According to Dante, it was the least dangerous sin, closest to heaven and farthest from the pit of hell. If we mean to ban medieval sins on the campus, we should reconsider sloth. We hardly know what the word means anymore. Laziness, people say. But sloth was far more invidious. It represented a kind of passivity that infected the soul so that the sinner was crippled by a *refusal of joy*.

As professors, we all have in our minds an ancient ideal of education, a joyful road of learning. This higher education deals with many of the horrors visited upon us as women and men, but then strives to reach beauty and pronounce a more positive celebration of learning. The ban on student-teacher relations is, finally, a broad attempt to poison the first adult experience for many young people—a complex, intimate, at times dangerous relationship with a grown-up who's not mom or dad. The ban's proponents refuse to recognize the broad spectrum of sexuality inherent on a campus; they would impose on all of us a withered sexuality that, like Milton's Satan in Paradise, is undelighted amid all delights.

11

College Professors Should Not Have Sexual Relations with Students

Martin Anderson

Martin Anderson was a senior adviser on the President's Economic Policy Advisory Board during the Reagan Administration. He is currently a senior fellow at the Hoover Institution at Stanford University in California.

As long as college professors are left unencumbered by regulations regarding sex with their students, a potential for the abuse of power and what some consider "authority rape" exists. The uneven power relationship between student and professor has created a situation where any argument supporting sexual relations between consenting adults (i.e., a professor and a student who is "of age") becomes specious. What is needed are policies promulgated by individual colleges and universities prohibiting student-faculty sexual relationships.

If there are any residual doubts about the low moral and intellectual state of universities, they should be erased by the growing debate about whether it is acceptable for professors to have sexual relationships with their students.

The simple fact that this is even disputed tells us how low some faculties have sunk.

Let's be clear about what is being debated. It isn't young love, an infatuation with an older professor; it isn't flirting and it isn't collegial companionship. It's whether it is okay for a professor to proposition a young student, or vice versa, and for them to have a sexual affair.

At issue is the potential for the abuse of power and authority. It is not a question of whether it is proper for professors to date students; it is a question of whether such activity is appropriate when both are at the same university or college.

For example, let's assume a young female student has enrolled in a course critical to her career. The professor, an older male, shows keen interest in his young pupil and brazenly asks her to sleep with him, clearly implying—but never saying so openly—that such activity can lead to

Martin Anderson, "College Professors Free to Proposition Students for Sex," *Human Events*, January 14, 1994. Reprinted with permission.

high grades and glowing letters of recommendation. The young woman agrees, the professor, true to his word, delivers on the grades and recommendations, and the student never complains.

Is this okay on today's campuses? Evidently so.

With a few notable exceptions, such conduct is condoned and rarely penalized. Some universities have officially sanctioned the conduct. This past fall [1993], Stanford University announced a new policy on sexual harassment that states: "The university has no formal policy prohibiting consensual romantic or sexual relationships among faculty, staff or students."

But all this may be changing. Student-professor sex, or what some might consider authority rape, is coming under increasing scrutiny.

The problem is primarily one of older male lechery. In their defense, they will argue piously that their students are "of age," that they are adults. That argument is specious and false.

At issue is the potential for the abuse of power and authority.

What really is involved here is the uneven power relationship between student and professor, in which the professor wields enormous authority over the student. The professor's power can be exercised subtly so that it is virtually impossible to detect malice when it is used to coerce or punish a reluctant student.

How widespread is student-professor sex? A 1988 survey of 235 male academics at a major research university yielded the interesting fact that 26% of them admitted having "had a sexual encounter or relationship with a student."

On a more personal note, listen to the words of a professor who participated in a discussion of this subject in the September 1993 issue of *Harper's* magazine.

Prof. William Kerrigan of the English department at the University of Massachusetts (Amherst) boasted that "I've had people take their clothes off in my office." He went on to explain that he was not defending "sex for grades" but that he had come across students in his career who were "working through something that only a professor could help her with."

"I'm talking about a female student who, for one reason or another, has unnaturally prolonged her virginity," explained Kerrigan, adding that, "There have been times when this virginity has been presented to me."

Prof. Kerrigan did acknowledge that "there often follows disappointment and, on the part of the student, anger," but argued that these relationships can be "very powerful sexually and psychologically, and because of that power, one can touch a student in a positive way."

Today only a handful of universities and colleges—Tufts University and Oberlin College, for example—have policies that prohibit student-professor sexual relationships and punish transgressors.

Tufts' policy is clear and direct: "It is a violation of university policy if a faculty member . . . engages in an amorous, dating or sexual relationship with a student whom he/she instructs, evaluates, supervises, advises."

Seems reasonable. But as long as schools like Tufts are the exception, the sick puppies of the academy are free to proposition their students at will, unimpeded by the slightest sanction from their peers.

12

Rape Should Be a Civil Rights Offense

Joseph R. Biden

Joseph R. Biden is a Democratic senator from Delaware and Chairman of the Committee on the Judiciary.

A six-month investigation of state rape prosecutions reveals an unconscionable disparity between how our system prosecutes rape and how it deals with other violent crimes. This disparity results from society's almost cavalier "boys will be boys" attitude toward the crime of rape. The Violence Against Women Act provides a civil rights remedy for victims of crimes related to gender. While this will not eliminate all violence against women, it elevates such offenses to a more visible, "first-class" status and thereby may provide the impetus to reverse a currently unacceptable situation.

The report I issue today culminates a 3-year investigation by the Judiciary Committee's majority staff concerning the causes and effects of violence against women. Women in America suffer all the crimes that plague the Nation—muggings, car thefts, and burglaries, to name a few. But there are also some crimes—namely, rape and family violence—that disproportionately burden women. Through a series of hearings and reports, the committee has studied this violence in an effort to determine what steps we can take to make women more safe.

Through this process, I have become convinced that violence against women reflects as much a failure of our Nation's collective moral imagination as it does the failure of our Nation's laws and regulations. We are helpless to change the course of this violence unless, and until, we achieve a national consensus that deserves our profound public outrage.

The report's findings

Today, the majority staff releases findings of a 6-month investigation of State rape prosecutions. These findings reveal a justice system that fails by any standard to meet its goals—apprehending, convicting, and incarcerating violent criminals:

- Ninety-eight percent of the victims of rape never see their attacker caught, tried and imprisoned;

Joseph R. Biden, Introduction to *The Response to Rape: Detours on the Road to Equal Justice*, a majority staff report prepared for the use of the Committee on the Judiciary, U.S. Senate, 103rd Cong., 1st sess., S. Print 103-147.

- Over half of all rape prosecutions are either dismissed before trial or result in an acquittal;
- Almost one-quarter of *convicted* rapists *never* go to prison; another quarter receive sentences in local jails *where the average sentence is 11 months:*

     This means that almost *half* of all *convicted* rapists can expect to serve an average of *a year or less* behind bars.

No crime carries a perfect record of arrest, prosecution, and incarceration, but the pattern that emerges for rape is strikingly inferior to that of other violent crimes:

- A robber is 30 percent more likely to be convicted than a rapist;
- A rape prosecution is more than twice as likely as a murder prosecution to be dismissed, and 30 percent more likely to be dismissed than a robbery prosecution; and,
- A convicted rapist is 50 percent more likely to receive probation than a convicted robber.

Imagine the public outcry if we were to learn today that one-quarter of convicted kidnappers or bank robbers were sentenced to probation or that 54 percent of arrests for these crimes never led to a conviction. We would consider such a system of justice inadequate to protect the Nation's property, yet we tolerate precisely such results when the rape of women is at issue.

The disparity in how our system prosecutes rape, in contrast to other violent crime, mirrors the disparity in our society's attitude toward these acts. The American legal system has always treated cases of assault by a stranger on our streets as a serious crime. But violence that primarily targets women has too often been dismissed without response. Where the victim knows the perpetrator, there is a tendency to consider the crime a product of a private relationship, not a matter of public injustice. Even where the violence comes at the hands of a stranger, the victim may be seen not as an innocent target of intolerable criminal acts, but as a participant who somehow bears shame or even some responsibility for the violence.

Violence against women reflects . . . a failure of our Nation's . . . moral imagination.

A recent case from New Jersey vividly illustrates this attitude. A 17-year-old mentally retarded girl was raped by a group of young men she had known her entire life, who used a baseball bat, a broom handle, and a stick to abuse her. This was not the furtive act of a lone individual, it was the afternoon activity of a group of young men who engaged in the rape of a girl as nonchalantly as a pickup game of basketball. After the crime became publicly known, members of the community, according to press accounts, defended the young men's conduct on the ground that "boys will be boys."

The nonchalance displayed by the young men during and after the attack reveals the attitude that this incident does not constitute serious criminal activity. Worst of all, this same attitude is mirrored in the court's treatment of the case. Although three of the defendants were convicted of first-degree aggravated sexual assault—the most serious charge under New Jersey law—and because of their age at the time of trial could have been sentenced as adults, the judge sentenced them as "youth offenders." As a result, they will likely serve less than 2 years in a youth camp. At sentencing, the judge made references to the attackers' status as successful high school athletes who presented "no threat" to society.

This is but one recent example of how our system discounts the severity of rape, how it "normalizes" rape as the mistakes of errant youth or negligent men. It is repeated day-in, day-out, in case after case, shaping women's perception that the system simply does not accept that violent acts against women are serious crimes. To reshape this perception, we must begin to ask the right questions:

- Why do we discount violence that occurs between people who know each other?
- Why do we seek to blame the victim for the rape—focusing on her behavior instead of her attacker's? Why is our system unresponsive to violence that occurs when a man terrorizes a woman through rape or other physical assault?

Survivors of rape and family violence pay a double price: like other victims of violent crime, they suffer the terrible toll of physical and psychological injury. But, unlike other crime victims, they also suffer the burden of defending the legitimacy of their suffering. It is bad enough when friends or neighbors ask why a survivor "let it happen," or why the survivor was in the "wrong place at the wrong time." But, when the criminal justice system adopts these attitudes of disbelief and hostility, the survivors' only recourse is to blame themselves.

More than any other factor, the attitude of our society that this violence is not serious stands in the way of reducing this violence. This attitude must change.

The first step in altering our attitudes toward this violence is to understand the failures of our laws and policies in this regard. Our criminal laws must be judged by their effectiveness in responding to the injustices done to victims of violence. This is the covenant of equal protection guaranteed by our Constitution—that our criminal justice system shall not make distinctions in practice that cannot be sustained in law. To fulfill this promise, we must put ourselves in the position of those who suffer this violence; we must use their experience as a measure of justice; and we must be vigilant in judging the laws as they operate in practice, as well as in theory.

The knowledge that society and its criminal justice system offer no real protection has the potential to victimize *all* women, forcing them to remain in abusive family situations, or to circumscribe their activities, to accept limitations on how they conduct their lives, because of fear. The stakes are high. If we do not succeed, we risk the faith of over half our citizens in the ability—and the willingness—of our criminal justice system to protect them. And, what is worse, we condemn future generations to accept not only the possibility of violence but the reality of lives too often limited by the fear of violence.

The Violence Against Women Act

To help focus the Nation's attention on this issue and to provide the help that survivors need, I first introduced the Violence Against Women Act in 1990. Since that time, I have chaired numerous hearings, heard from scores of women who have suffered violence, and released a number of reports documenting our findings. This year, I have introduced the bill for what I hope is the last time—it is my highest legislative priority to see S. 11 become law during this Congress.

The legislation is the first comprehensive approach to fighting all forms of violence against women, combining a broad array of needed reforms. These include:

- New laws to reinforce the focus on the offender's conduct, rather than the victim's character;
- New investments in local law enforcement efforts that treat rape and family violence as serious crime;
- New evidentiary rules that extend "rape shield"–type protection to civil and criminal cases as well as sex harassment litigation; and
- New education programs in our schools and in our law enforcement institutions about family violence and rape.

Most importantly, in my view, the Violence Against Women Act creates, for the first time, a civil rights remedy for victims of crimes "motivated by gender." I believe this provision is the key to changing the attitudes about violence against women. This provision recognizes that violent crimes committed because of a person's gender raise issues of equality as well as issues of safety and accountability. Long ago, we recognized that an individual who is attacked because of his race is deprived of his right to be free and equal; we should guarantee the same protection for victims who are attacked *because* of their gender. Whether the violence is motivated by racial bias or ethnic bias or gender bias, the law's protection should be the same.

I realize that this legislation will not eradicate violence against women, but I do believe that it is a step in the right direction—in the direction of changing this Nation's "false idea" that violence directed at women is "second-class" crime. Until we recognize that fact and brand the violence as brutal and wrong, we can never hope to stem the tide of violence against women in America.

Conclusion

The purpose of this report is to help us recognize that "violence against women" is simply "violence." *We are all responsible for the beliefs and the attitudes that allow us to apply rape laws grudgingly, with suspicion rather than sympathy.* As the Attorney General recently reminded us during her confirmation hearings, the doors of the Justice Department offer the following reminder to all who enter: "Justice in the Life and Conduct of the State is possible only as first it resides in the Heart and Souls of the Citizens." It is my hope that this report, with the others released by the committee on this subject, will move our hearts and souls and, in doing so, will help us to create a system that realizes the promise of equal justice for all.

13

Rape Should Not Be a Civil Rights Offense

Neil Gilbert

Neil Gilbert is a professor of social welfare at the University of California, Berkeley.

The Violence Against Women Act of 1993 (which was recently enacted as part of the Senate's 1993–1994 Omnibus Crime Bill) classifies rape motivated by gender bias as a civil rights offense. The authors of the bill erroneously claim that in the area of violent crime, rape results in the lowest number of convictions and incarcerations. In fact, the conviction and incarceration rates for robbery, aggravated assault, and other violent crimes approximate those of rape. The reality is that the United States Senate has reacted to the shrill and exaggerated claims of victimization by radical feminists.

The Senate Judiciary Committee has answered the dreams of radical feminist lawyers with its proposed Violence Against Women Act of 1993, which would classify rape motivated by gender bias as a civil rights offense under which victims could sue for compensatory and punitive damages. The act also earmarks $85 million to rape crisis centers for education and prevention services to deal with an epidemic of date rape that does not really exist, but is likely to be spawned by linking rape to civil rights and punitive damages.

The argument for making rape a civil rights offense and granting millions to rape crisis centers is detailed in the Judiciary Committee's majority staff report, *The Response to Rape: Detours on the Road to Equal Justice.* As the title suggests, the staff's analysis charges that rape victims do not receive equal justice under the current law. Their case rests on findings of inequality between rape and other violent crimes related to rates of convictions, dismissals and reporting. Following the tendency of most documents that advocate for a cause, this report furnishes a highly one-sided reading of the evidence, relying on vivid anecdotes to support fragile numbers.

Two of the principal claims, repeated several times throughout the report, are that 84% of reported rapes never result in a conviction and that in 88% of reported rapes the assailant is not incarcerated. We are also in-

Neil Gilbert, "The Wrong Response to Rape," *The Wall Street Journal*, June 29, 1993. Reprinted with permission of *The Wall Street Journal*, ©1993 Dow Jones & Company, Inc. All rights reserved.

formed that while less than half of all individuals arrested for rape are convicted, more than 60% of those arrested for robbery are convicted. All this is true. Whether it reflects unequal justice is another matter.

The numbers in perspective

What the report does not tell us is that, using exactly the same computations on the data from the same sources, 87% of reported robberies never result in a conviction and in 89% of reported robberies the assailant is not incarcerated. The overall conviction rates are roughly the same for aggravated assault and somewhat lower for the nonviolent crime of burglary. Although the report provides only the numbers that intimate an alarming inequality of justice, the fact is that among the violent crimes of rape, robbery and aggravated assault, the relation between reported crimes and convictions is equally deplorable.

Compared with the data on reported cases of robbery, the data on reported rapes reveal both a higher percentage of arrests and a higher percentage of dismissals before coming to trial. Dismissals before trial are commonly the result of weak evidence or the victim's refusal to testify. According to the staff's analysis, however, "in rape cases there is another factor at work." That is, the victims are often acquainted with their molesters.

The report cites evidence that prosecutors hesitate to bring any case to trial—whether it be a robbery case, an assault case, or a kidnapping case—in which the offender knew the victim. In light of this tendency, the report speculates that proportionately more rapes (48%) than robberies (37%) are dismissed not because the evidence might have been weak or because the victims decided not to testify, but because in a very high proportion of reported cases the offender was not a stranger.

It is true that many victims of rape know their assailants, but so do the victims of other violent crimes (a point the reports fails to convey). Indeed, according to the Bureau of Justice Statistics' figures for 1989 and 1990, the proportion of victims reporting robberies and aggravated assaults who were acquainted with their offenders was as high as—if not higher than—those for reported rapes. Although dismissal rates vary, once the cases make it to the courtroom the conviction rates for rape and robbery are almost equal.

The answer is not to make rape a civil rights offense.

Finally, claims about unequal rates of arrest and convictions for rapists are magnified by the issue of unreported cases. Another reflection of what is said to be the unequal justice afforded women is the fact that many, if not most, rapes go unreported. No one really knows the number of these unreported cases. But we are informed by the Judiciary Committee staff that "according to a conservative estimates, as many as 84% of rapes each year are never reported." They explain in a footnote that this estimate is "conservative" when compared with figures presented by University of Arizona Prof. Mary Koss, who directed the *Ms.* Magazine Campus Project on Sexual Assault.

Prof. Koss's widely publicized figures showed that 27% of college women were victims of rape or attempted rape an average of two times between the ages of 14 and 21. The problem with this study is that 73%

of the college women whom Prof. Koss classified as victims did not think they had been raped; more than 40% went back and had sex again with the man who Prof. Koss believed raped them. Most of the college women in Prof. Koss's study probably counted themselves as feminists, but to the radical fringe they are rape victims who (like the male targets of fringe criticism) "just don't get it." Next to this study, almost any research on rape looks conservative.

There are several problems with the so-called conservative estimate of unreported rapes drawn by the Judiciary Committee staff from a study entitled *Rape in America*, conducted by the National Victim Center and the Crime Victims Research and Treatment Center. Based on the results of a national survey, the study estimates that 683,000 women are victims of rape each year. The survey sample was scientifically designed to allow for valid generalizations to the broader population. But the accuracy of these generalizations is seriously undermined by the fact that almost one-third of the scientifically designed sample did not participate in the second wave of interviews, from which the annual incidence rate of rape was calculated.

The 3,220 study participants interviewed during the second wave amounted to only 68% of the original sample. With a sample this size, the nationwide estimate of 683,000 rapes was based on 23 cases of rape uncovered in the interviews.

For a truly conservative estimate of unreported rape cases the Judiciary Committee staff could have turned to the findings of the Bureau of Justice Statistics' surveys, actually conducted by the Census Bureau, which involve a random sample of about 62,000 households interviewed every six months, with response rates of more than 90%. The BJS findings reveal that in 1989 and 1990 almost half of their respondents who were victims of rape did not report this crime to the police. Although this figure is lower than the 84% of unreported cases cited in the Judiciary Committee's staff report, it is no trivial matter. Once again, however, on this score rape victims do not differ from victims of other violent crimes. According to the BJS data, 49% of robbery cases and 43% of aggravated assault cases were not reported to the police during this period,

The BJS studies, of course, are not free of methodological problems. They have been widely criticized for underestimating the incidence of rape. But as Christopher Jencks notes, since the BJS surveys are conducted almost the same way every year, their biases are likely to be constant—so these figures provide a reliable guide to trends in violent crime over time. In this regard it is worth noting that the BJS data show the rates of rape declining about 30% between 1980 and 1990.

Insufferable norms

The good news in all these numbers is that regarding rates of arrests, convictions, dismissals and reportings, victims of rape are not treated any less equally than other crime victims. Despite the claims in the Judiciary Committee's staff report, the evidence does not demonstrate a "consistent pattern that diverges from the norm." The unfortunate news is that justice is appallingly thin all about—for all victims the norms are insufferable.

But the answer is not to make rape a civil rights offense. This would lower the threshold of proof in rape cases, introduce psychological issues of motivation, and provide a huge financial incentive for expanding the definition of rape (in line with the radical feminist agenda) to include all sorts of ambiguous or unpleasant sexual experiences. The big winners in all this would of course be the lawyers and the therapists. Nor is equal justice advanced by giving rape crisis centers $85 million to combat an epidemic that does not exist.

The act is designed to promote the cause of radical feminists, whose exaggerated claims of victimization deserve the critical scrutiny they are just beginning to receive from moderate feminists. If the Judiciary Committee's aim is to champion the cause of equal justice for all citizens, these funds can be better spent to improve our courts and to increase the number of police protecting our communities.

Organizations to Contact

The editors have compiled the following list of organizations concerned with the issues debated in this book. The descriptions are derived from materials provided by the organizations. All have publications or information available for interested readers. The list was compiled on the date of publication of the present volume; names, addresses, and phone numbers may change. Be aware that many organizations take several weeks or longer to respond to inquiries, so allow as much time as possible.

American Association of University Professors (AAUP)
1012 14th St. NW
Washington, DC 20005
(202) 737-5900
fax (202) 737-5526

The AAUP which is made up of college and university professors, research scholars, and academic librarians, aims to facilitate cooperation among teachers and research scholars for the promotion of higher education, research, and the ideals of the profession. This organization can provide information on sexual harassment policies at colleges and universities. It publishes the *Academe: Bulletin of the AAUP*, a magazine that discusses association business and issues in higher education.

American College Health Association (ACHA)
PO Box 28937
Baltimore, MD 21240-8937
(410) 859-1500
fax (410) 859-1510

This organization works with higher education institutions to promote health in its broadest aspects for students and all other members of the college community. ACHA compiles statistics and publishes numerous publications on student health issues, including acquaintance rape and sexually transmitted diseases. It publishes the brochure *Acquaintance Rape*.

Association of Governing Boards of Universities and Colleges (AGB)
1 Dupont Circle NW, Suite 400
Washington, DC 20036
(202) 296-8400
fax (202) 223-7053

The association includes governing boards of public and private 2- and 4-year colleges and universities. It addresses the problems and responsibilities of trusteeship in all sectors of higher education and the relationships of trustees and regents to the president, the faculty, and the student body. It publishes the *AGB Report*, a newsletter that focuses on issues and trends in higher education, as well as *"No Means No": Sexual Harassment and Date Rape*, a study for the development of date rape policies on university and college campuses.

Campus Violence Prevention Center
Towson State University
Towson, MD 21204-7097
(410) 830-2055

This research center conducts national surveys of such campus issues as date rape, campus violence, and alcohol consumption. It has two publications, *Responding to Violence on Campus*, a source book of papers presented at various conferences, and *The Links Among Alcohol, Drugs, and Crime on American College Campuses*, a book based on national surveys.

Center for Women's Policy Studies (CWPS)
2000 P St. NW, Suite 508
Washington, DC 20036
(202) 872-1770

CWPS is an independent feminist policy research and advocacy institution established in 1972. The center studies policies affecting the social, legal, health, and economic status of women. It publishes the booklets *Campus Gang Rape* and *Campus Sexual Harassment*, as well as reports on a variety of topics related to women's equality and empowerment, including sexual harassment, campus rape, and violence against women.

Columbia University Center on Addiction and Substance Abuse
152 W. 57th St., 12th Floor
New York, NY 10019

The center conducts research related to substance abuse and addiction. In its June 1994 report, *Rethinking Rites of Passage: Substance Abuse on America's Campuses*, a panel found that 90 percent of all reported campus rapes take place when the assailant or victim is using alcohol.

National Association of College and University Attorneys (NACUA)
1 Dupont Circle, Suite 620
Washington, DC 20036
(202) 833-8390
fax (202) 296-8379

The association represents approximately 1300 U.S. and Canadian campuses and 650 colleges and universities in legal matters. It compiles and distributes legal decisions, opinions, and other writings and information on legal problems affecting colleges and universities. Publications include *Acquaintance Rape on Campus: A Model for Institutional Response* and *Crime on Campus*.

National Coalition of Free Men
PO Box 129
Manhasset, NY 11030
(516) 482-6378

The coalition's members include men seeking a "fair and balanced perspective on gender issues." The organization promotes the legal rights of men in issues of abortion, divorce, false accusation of rape, sexual harassment, and sexual abuse. It conducts research, sponsors education programs, maintains a database on men's issues, and publishes the bimonthly *Transitions*.

National Organization for Women Legal Defense and Education Fund
99 Hudson St.
New York, NY 10013
(212) 925-6635
fax (212) 226-1066

The fund provides legal referrals and conducts research on a broad range of issues concerning women and the law. It offers a comprehensive list of publications, including testimony on sexual harassment, books, articles, reports, and briefs. The fund offers legal resource kits pertaining to a variety of issues, including violence against women.

National Victims Resource Center (NVRC)
Box 6000
Rockville, MD 20850
(800) 627-6872

Established in 1983 by the U.S. Department of Justice's Office for Victims of Crime, NVRC is a primary source of information regarding victim-related issues. The center answers questions by using national and regional statistics, a comprehensive collection of research findings, and a well-established network of victim advocates and organizations. NVRC distributes all Office of Justice Programs (OJP) publications, including *Female Victims of Violent Crime* and *Sexual Assault: An Overview*.

People Against Rape (PAR)
PO Box 5318
River Forest, IL 60305
(800) 877-7252

People Against Rape primarily seeks to help teens and children avoid becoming the victims of sexual assault and rape by providing instruction in the basic principles of self-defense. PAR further promotes self-esteem and motivation of teens and college students through educational programs. Publications include *Defend: Preventing Date Rape and Other Sexual Assaults* and *Sexual Assault: How to Defend Yourself*.

Women Against Pornography (WAP)
PO Box 845, Times Square Station
New York, NY 10036-0845

WAP is a feminist organization that seeks to change public opinion about pornography so that Americans no longer view it as socially acceptable or sexually liberating. It offers tours of New York's Times Square that are intended to show firsthand that "the essence of pornography is about the degradation, objectification, and brutalization of women." WAP offers slide shows, lectures, and a referral service to victims of sexual abuse and sexual exploitation. Its publications include *Women Against Pornography—Newsreport*.

Bibliography

Books

Julie A. Allison and Lawrence S. Wrightman	*Rape: The Misunderstood Crime.* Newbury Park, CA: Sage Publications, 1993.
Sari Knopp Biklen and Diane Pollard, eds.	*Gender and Education.* Chicago: National Society for the Study of Education Yearbook, 1993.
Carol Bohmer and Andrea Parrot	*Sexual Assault on Campus: The Problem and the Solution.* New York: Lexington Books, 1993.
Emilie Buchwald, Pamela Fletcher, and Martha Roth, eds.	*Transforming a Rape Culture.* Minneapolis: Milkweed Editions, 1993.
Billie Wright Dziech and Linda Weiner	*The Lecherous Professor: Sexual Harassment on Campus.* Champaign: University of Illinois Press, 1992.
Joel Friedman et al.	*Date Rape: What It Is, What It Isn't, What It Does to You, What You Can Do About It.* Deerfield Beach, FL: Health Communications, 1992.
Michele A. Paludi and Richard B. Barickman	*Academic and Workplace Sexual Harassment: A Resource Manual.* Albany: State University of New York Press, 1992.
Robert O. Riggs, Patricia H. Murrell, and JoAnn C. Cutting	*Sexual Harassment in Higher Education.* Washington: George Washington University, 1993.
Katie Roiphe	*The Morning After: Sex, Fear, and Feminism.* Boston: Little, Brown & Company, 1993.
Peggy Reeves Sanday	*Fraternity Gang Rape: Sex, Brotherhood, and Privilege on Campus.* New York: New York University Press, 1990.
Robin Warshaw	*I Never Called It Rape: The* Ms. *Report on Recognizing, Fighting and Surviving Date and Acquaintance Rape.* New York: HarperPerennial, 1994.

Periodicals

Andy Abrams and Kristine Herman	"Antioch Is Not Legislating Sexual Correctness," *The Chronicle of Higher Education,* January 26, 1994.
Ronet Bachman, Sally Ward, and Raymond Paternoster	"The Rationality of Sexual Offending: Testing a Deterrence/Rational Choice Conception of Sexual Assault," *Law & Society Review,* vol. 26, no. 2, 1992.
Doris Bacon and E. Ashley, eds.	"Rape and Denial," *People Weekly,* August 16, 1993.
B. Bergman	"Conflict on Campus," *Maclean's,* November 29, 1993
Connie L. Best, Bonnie S. Dansky, and Dean G. Kilpatrick	"Medical Students' Attitudes About Female Rape Victims," *Journal of Interpersonal Violence,* June 1992. Available from Sage Publications, 2455 Teller Rd. Newbury Park, CA 91320.

Margaret D. Bonilla   "Cultural Assault: What Feminists Are Doing to Rape Ought to Be a Crime," *Policy Review*, Fall 1993.

T.D. Bostwick and   "Effects of Gender and Specific Dating Behaviors on
J.L. Delucia   Perceptions of Sex Willingness and Date Rape," *Journal of Social and Clinical Psychology*, Spring 1992. Available from Guilford Publications, 72 Spring St., New York, NY 10012.

Eileen C. Brady et al.   "Date Rape: Expectations, Avoidance Strategies, and Attitudes Toward Victims," *Journal of Social Psychology*, June 1991. Available from Heldref Publications, 1319 18th St. NW, Washington, DC 20036-1802.

J.S. Bridges   "Perceptions of Date and Stranger Rape: A Difference in Sex Role Expectations and Rape-Supportive Beliefs," *Sex Roles*, March 1991.

S.L. Caron and   "Rape Sexual Assault on the College Campus: Some
L. Brossoit   Questions to Think About," *Journal of College Student Development*, March 1992. Available from 5999 Stevenson Ave., Alexandria, VA 22304.

William Celis III   "Growing Talk of Date Rape Separates Sex from Assault," *The New York Times*, January 2, 1991.

Jeffrey K. Clark   "Complications in Academia: Sexual Harassment and the Law," *SIECUS Report*, August/September 1993. Available from 130 W. 42nd St., Suite 2500, New York, NY 10036.

Shawn Corne, John   "Women's Attitudes and Fantasies About Rape as a
Briere, and Lillian M.   Function of Early Exposure to Pornography," *Journal
Esses   of Interpersonal Violence*, December 1992.

CQ Researcher   "Sex on Campus," November 4, 1994. Available from 1414 22nd St. NW, Washington, DC 20037.

M. Esselman and   "Silent Screams," *People Weekly*, June 20, 1994.
E. Velez

Edward Felsenthal   "The Risk of Lawsuits Disheartens Colleges Fighting Date Rape," *The Wall Street Journal*, April 12, 1994.

Eric Felten   "A Redefinition of the Issue of Rape," *Insight on the News*, January 28, 1991. Available from 3600 New York Ave. NE, Washington, DC 20002.

Suzanne Fields   "Rape as Sport: The Culture Is at the Root," *Insight on the News*, May 3, 1993.

C. Finney and   "Rape on Campus: The Prevalence of Sexual Assault
E. Corty   While Enrolled in College," *Journal of College Student Development*, March 1993.

Neil Gilbert   "The Campus Rape Scare," *The Wall Street Journal*, June 27, 1991.

Neil Gilbert   "Was It Rape? An Examination of Sexual Abuse Statistics," *The American Enterprise*, September/October 1994.

Jeff Giles   "There's a Time for Talk, and a Time for Action," *Newsweek*, March 7, 1994.

Sarah Glazer	"Date Rape: A Campus Obsession?" *Glamour*, June 1993.
Laurel Graeber	"Sexual Beasts vs. Delicate Vessels: Sex, Fear, and Feminism on Campus," *New York Times Book Review*, September 19, 1993.
Richard Grenier	"Some Advice on Consent: This Is Going Way Too Far," *Insight on the News*, November 1, 1993.
Stephanie Gutmann	"Are All Men Rapists?" *National Review*, August 23, 1993.
Harper's Magazine	"New Rules About Sex on Campus," September 1993.
Peter Hellman	"Crying Rape: The Politics of Rape on Campus," *New York*, March 8, 1993.
Kathleen Hirsch	"Fraternities of Fear: Gang Rape, Male Bonding, and the Silencing of Women," *Ms.*, September/October 1990.
D.N. Husak and G.C. Thomas	"Date Rape, Social Convention, and Reasonable Mistakes," *Law and Philosophy*, 1992.
G. David Johnson, Gloria J. Palileo, and Norma B. Gray	"Date Rape on a Southern Campus: Reports from 1991," *Sociology and Social Research*, January 1992.
J. Kasindorf	"Inside the Mind of a Rapist," *Redbook*, January 1993.
Katherine C. Kormos and Charles I. Brooks	"Acquaintance Rape: Attributions of Victim Blame by College Students and Prison Inmates as a Function of Relationship Status of Victim and Assailant," *Psychological Reports*, April 1994. Available from Box 9229, Missoula, MT 59807.
Mary P. Koss	"Defending Date Rape," *Journal of Interpersonal Violence*, March 1992.
Cindi Leive	"The Dangerous Truth About Acquaintance Rape," *Glamour*, June 1993.
G.O. Lenihan et al.	"Gender Differences in Rape Supportive Attitudes Before and After a Date Rape Education Intervention," *Journal of College Student Development*, July 1992.
Ronald B. Lieber	"Call the Police, Not the Dean," *The New York Times*, September 11, 1991.
Cathi Dunn MacRae	"Straight Talk About Date Rape," *Wilson Library Bulletin*, November 1993. Available from 950 University Ave., Bronx, NY 10452.
Anne Matthews	"The Campus Crime Wave," *The New York Times Magazine*, March 7, 1993.
K. McLendon	"Male and Female Perceptions of Date Rape," *Journal of Social Behavior and Personality*, September 1994. Available from Select Press, PO Box 37, Corte Madera, CA 94976.
Crystal S. Mills and Barbara J. Granoff	"Date and Acquaintance Rape Among a Sample of College Students," *Social Work*, November 1992.
R. Proite, M. Dannells, and S.L. Benton	"Gender, Sex-Role Stereotypes, and the Attribution of Responsibility for Date and Acquaintance Rape," *Journal of College Student Development*, November 1993.

Katie Roiphe

"Date Rape Hysteria," *The New York Times Magazine*, November, 29, 1991.

Ruth Schmidt

"After the Fact: To Speak of Rape," *The Christian Century*, January 6–13, 1993.

C. SerVaas

"Easing Woes for Rape Victims," *The Saturday Evening Post*, May/June 1993.

Ruth Shalit

"Radical Exhibitionists," *Reason*, July 1992.

E.R. Shipp

"Bearing Witness to the Unbearable," *The New York Times*, July 28, 1991.

Toby Simon

"Sexuality on Campus: '90s Style," *Change*, September 1993.

Judith Stone

"Sex, Rape and Second Thoughts," *Glamour*, October 1993.

Lynda A. Szymanski et al.

"Gender Role and Attitudes Toward Rape in Male and Female College Students," *Sex Roles*, July 1993.

Diana Trilling

"My Turn," *Newsweek*, June 6, 1994.

S. Youngwood and C. Hoyt

"Rape: How to Protect Yourself," *McCall's,* April 1993.

Index